WINNER

CHANGING LIGHT
NOVEL-IN-VERSE

FIND YOUR OWN

WAY HOME

Michael George

Livingston Press

University of West Alabama

Library of Congress Control Number: 2024935762

Typesetting and page layout: Joe Taylor, Eleanor Boudreau
Proofreading: Brooke Barger, Eleanor Boudreau, Savannah Beams,
Tricia Taylor

Cover layout and art: Grace Deerman

***This work won the Changing Light
Novel-in-Verse contest, judged by Eleanor Boudreau***

Acknowledgements
Many thanks to Janet Hutchings, editor of EQMM, for publishing "Bad
Boy" as a stand-alone verse story and showing enthusiasm for the Find Your Own Way
Home manuscript. Thank you also to early readers, including Julia Burns, Fred Dale,
and Clark Lunberry. I value your insights more than you can know. Joe Taylor and
Eleanor Boudreau at Livingston Press are champions of the multi-form, the offbeat,
and the risky, and they have been wonderful to work with. My enduring gratitude to
them for awarding Find Your Own Way Home the Changing Light Prize and giving
the book a loving home.

FIND YOUR OWN

WAY HOME

Commit a crime, and the world is made of glass.

– Ralph Waldo Emerson

BAD BOY

1

                        They call

me Bad Boy, racing around town

the way I do, the town worth racing,

bumping shoulders on the signs

that say just what they mean—*First Bank,*

like there's a second?—*Bouquet Florist,*

'cause you can't afford a vase?—

Block City Pizza, 'cause they don't

have paint to paint the cinderblocks?—

and *Bob's Used Auto Sales* and *Buy-*

Me Discount Furniture, which tells

you all you need to know. And me?

Bad Boy because I ain't no good.

A dustball cheapskate town and Broad

Street much the way is just two lanes,

which goes to show you what broad counts

for here—and Hollow Rock is Nowhere

Tennessee, but, like they say,

it's home—which is the reason why

I put a big-block V-8 in

my '72 Chevelle—the reason,

come midnight when the hollow sounds

like some disease has done its work—

and all the houses empty, all

the people dead—I light the fuse

and race up Seminary Street,

across Old Pisgah Road, around

back southward over the Hollow Rock

Branch railroad tracks a hundred miles

an hour—my tires leave asphalt and

I fly. Watch me—I fly.

                                        I stocked

the shelves at Hometown Market till

they locked the doors, and then I washed

the kettles at The Iron Kettle,

then cut the grass at Prospect Baptist—

but lately I'd been sleeping in

and thinking about my future, which

looked hungry. Bondo was the plan.

If Bob would go in halves, I'd fix,

he'd sell.

          Then Tommy took up cooking

until his Shake-and-Bake exploded

Michael George

high to Kingdom Come—and when

the doctors kicked him out, his skin

looked like a python's on the day

it sheds, which made me think life's short

and auto body's a fool's slog.

A boy like me needs quick.

On Friday nights that autumn,

when Tommy could go out again,

we drove to Central High and watched

the Tigers beat the mangy fur

off Collinwood, McEwen, Gleason.

Tommy, who still wore sunglasses

at night—because his corneas—

danced in the stands, his Ray Charles teeth,

cheerleaders flipping, tumbling, yelling

the things they yell.

That's when

I saw her slip behind the stands,

her back to all that sound—and I

told Tommy, *Find your own ride home,*

and down I went and never came

back up for air until West Memphis,

where I got too much of it.

The girl was crying, sitting on

the yellow dirt, her arms around

her knees, pink high-top sneakers loose,

like she was sinking. *Why?* I said.

The look she gave me—I could skate

across those eyes.

She said,

The world is sad—Can't a girl cry?

I said, *The Tigers up Eight-O,*

the world is sad? The moon so high—

The stars? Because I talk that way.

She said, *You talk real dumb.* I said,

It's how I talk when I'm in love.

In Hollow Rock a line like that

gets *A* for effort, even if

a girl thinks you're a douche. *My name,*

she said, *is Alison.* I said,

I won't forget that name. Not ever.

2

        No one much minded

how we went together—a girl

like Alison, who cried, a boy

like me. Good for each other, that's

what people said. Sometimes love happens

early—you're lucky if it happens

ever, some folks lonely first

to last.

        Now when I touched the gas

and raced up Seminary Street,

Alison sat beside me, window

open, the night air howling in,

forgetting all I didn't know

till then I wanted to forget—

or parked outside her grandma's house

on Holcomb. Windows up against

the coming cold, she said, *You ever*

think of leaving? I said, *Nope.*

The truth was, right there in the car

with her was where I thought I'd be

if everything worked out, a boy

like me who knew how engines worked.

I could've told her that I knew

every road in Hollow Rock

and that I closed my eyes on High

Street, blindly driving all its bends

like windings in my dreams. I could've

said I was a dustball boy

and dustball boys like dustball towns.

I could've told her flying off

the Hollow Rock Branch railroad tracks

a hundred miles an hour was far

enough and high as I would go.

She said, *I think of leaving all*

the time. And I said, *Don't.* She held

to me. I held to her. You can't

blame kids for dancing that way, holding

each other like they'll fall, feet shuffling

on wooden floors. She held and said,

You ever think of how you want

to die? You want to see it coming?

You want it fast—or slow? You want

a friend there with you? Want to be

alone? I said, *No, Alison,*

I never think of that.

3

           After the blow-up,

Tommy quit his cooking, started

Sundays at Prospect Baptist, cutting

the grass from goodness of his heart.

But boys need something to repent of.

Friday nights when football ended,

Tommy's uncle dug a fire

pit in his yard, and you could pay

ten bucks or bring your own. Then Fridays

turned to Thursdays, Tuesdays too,

and soon the party never stopped,

and if you passed out, Tommy's uncle

dragged your ass, but if you paid

your ten bucks or your bottle, you

might never go back home.

Then Alison said, *School's for losers—*

Look at you. She had a point.

We more or less camped out at Uncle's

until her grandma called the law—

the county sheriff pulled his car

under the pines, and huffed and puffed,

came inside without knocking, found us

in Uncle's dirty bed, and said,

She's fifteen, son—That's rape.

I said, *No, sir, it's love.* He said,

We don't distinguish in this county—

but if you run, and I mean run,

I might not shoot you in the back.

A long, long time ago, I was

a young man too—I don't forget.

So it was back to Central High

for her and sleeping in for me.

They told me, *Stay away.* And *Nothing*

good can come. And *Crying's normal,*

a girl her age. And *If it's real,*

it's real, so why you rushing? Told me,

Speeding boys like you must learn

to take it slow. They said, *You stay*

a hundred yards, not an inch less.

They said, *We'll only tell you once,*

then told me it again. I listened

to them about a week—then drove

past Grandma's house at midnight, past

again at dawn.

November turned

December and the wind got cold.

I bought a case of Bondo, made

a yard sign, no one came. I drove

past Grandma's house at midnight. Tommy

mainlined hydrocodone and

the Afghan hash his brother brought

back when he came home crippled, and

I passed again at dawn—the shades

down always, the rocking chair in front,

the swinging chains. I called her number—

It rang. I took to sitting in

my Chevy outside Central High

at three p.m. I tell you—I

don't mind who knows—I had it bad.

A girl like Alison you don't

find at the Carroll County Fair.

She's like a light you see at night

too low on the horizon and

you think you see an airplane crashing—

you listen for the sound and hear

none, turn on the TV and there's

no news, and then you wonder what

you saw and did you even see it?—

something bright and terrible,

the beauty hurts your eyes, you only

wish you'd see it once again.

The night the ground first froze, she left

her bedroom window open just

for me. I hit the gas and woke

the neighborhood from Bruceton clear

to Hamilton—the nighttime rang,

it surely rang.

4

Christmas in Hollow Rock's a singing

season and the earth is brown.

If you want diamonds from the sky,

squint at the stars and cry—the coldest

nights are clearest. Not fifteen miles

to Janice's Jewels and Watches Store.

A plated bracelet, just eight bucks,

an emerald ring, eight hundred ten.

I bought a golden droplet necklace,

ninety down and monthly payments.

Christmas Eve, my Chevy idling

low like *ho, ho, ho*, I ran

across her lawn, her window wide

and set the box down on the sill.

The bedroom air smelled like she did,

that kind of tenderness no one

has named except to call it tender,

a kind of easy breathing.

Her voice thrilled me like flying, said,

from somewhere in the black, *You aim*

to stand outside all night, you fool?

I scrambled through the window like

the lawn on fire, my Chevy idling

ho, ho, ho-ing at the streetside—

It idled all night long.

Oh, Grandma didn't get the joke.

First light she thumped the bedroom door—

her Christmas cheer all Christmas blue—

said, *Merry . . . what in Jesus's name?*

I was a stocking filled with coal.

I said, *Old lady, where's the spirit?*

She said, *They're serving it in jail.*

Ho, ho, I said, *a good one, Granny.*

She said, *Stay right here while I fetch*

my gun.

Back out the window—tailing

bare-assed hot across the lawn—

the V-8 thrumming—I felt blessed.

I tell you, Alison was something

missing, something I had missed

my whole life, never knew I'd missed

until I found her—Alison,

a girl who cried behind the bleachers

because the world is sad and smelled

like tenderness and something no

one's named.

5

Tommy said, *Boy, you're pussy-whipped.*

I said, *You want to see the stripes?*

He said, *It can't end good, a girl*

so young. I said, *So what's your cocktail—*

heroin this week? He said,

I'm only saying. I said, *Don't.*

The sheriff couldn't scare me if

he couldn't catch me—Alison,

a ghost who passed from windows on

the coldest nights of January

like a frozen breath. We drove

by Nebo Baptist where they shined

the lights, out Roundhouse Road, and through

the park gates where nobody picnics

anymore. In Tennessee,

in winter dark, the wind is still,

the branches silent in the trees—

and some nights we were silent as

the trees and listened to that silence

as cold seeped through the car—some nights

she said, *You ever want to go?*

And I said, *No, I like it right*

here by your side. And dawn comes late

in January.

Some nights she climbed

onto my lap and breathed her ghost

breath in my mouth, and if we'd gone

down under the earth's surface I

believe we could've lived like that

for months or years, breathing each other.

Grandma got crazy—you could call

it jealousy, that's what it looked like.

I dropped off Alison a block

or two from home—she stumbled past

the cherry tops—said to the cops,

I went out walking, Deputy Dogs,

that's all—a girl can walk, can't she?

You got a law against a girl like me?

Then Grandma threatened fire—and all

the neighbors pulling down their shades.

The snow fell, footprints on

the windshield, soft as beetles, and

I turned the headlights on and said,

Why don't you marry me? She laughed

the way she cried, mostly without

a sound and mostly with the eyes.

I said, *You know me—I ain't joking.*

She said, *There's world enough,* and climbed

onto my lap and breathed and breathed.

6

In February, I was broke.

No one was hiring boys that screwed

young girls. I got a reputation,

never ducked. Then Tommy said,

I'll set you up—sweet car like yours,

you'll roll the life from ATM

to ATM. I said, *Are you*

still molting? Do you ever get

a good night's sleep? What would

you say your pain is—scale of one

to ten? Eleven? No, I'll drive

it down the dotted line.

But broke is broke, and so

I went to Huntington and robbed

the Rite Aid Pharmacy—enough

for food and gas, enough to keep

the power and heat on, like they say.

The sheriff came by when he saw

the video. He said, *A boy*

that looks an awful lot like you

done something bad. The clerk, who knows?—

The doctors say it's touch and go.

I said, *A boy that doesn't wear*

a mask and gloves deserves what comes.

He cracked his cracker knuckles—*Where*

were you today 'round three? I said,

This pretty face needs rest. I stay

in bed till four. He said, *No one*

in bed with you to testify?

I said, *You'd bust me if she was.*

He said, *I close my eyes too much*

to boys like you. Next time I see

you where you don't belong, I'll grind

that pretty face into the stone.

Get back on your horse or never ride—

Or is it, Learn from past mistakes?

Next day I drove across the line

to Jackson and I robbed the Walgreens.

I broke the glass display and took

the Sudafed for Tommy just

because I could. I grabbed a box

of Russell Stover chocolates too—

Valentine's Day was coming—a heart

box, red as sundown, big as the rising

moon. At midnight in the park,

she said, *You shouldn't have*. I said,

That's probably true.

Fred's Pharmacy in Camden had

a special on cough medicine—

Delsym and Tylenol for Cold

and Flu. All I could carry—buy

none, get ten free.

           Now Tommy cooked

and cooked—the boy was a volcano.

Along the road beyond his driveway,

blackened tweaker teeth crunched tires

like gravel. All that February

you breathed ammonia. Speed freaks lined

up at his house— we called it Dunkin'—

bags of crank instead of glazed.

I paid my bill at Janice's Jewels

four months early. If truth is true,

I sampled some—and brushed my teeth

twice after. If truth is true, I liked

it some—the way my Chevy lifted

at railroad crossings, hundred miles

an hour—and flew. I never was

a student, never cared for math,

but just one hit of Tommy's crystal

multiplied that hundred miles

an hour by ten and if you saw

a rocket ship in Hollow Rock

that rocket ship was me.

7

You ever hear a story like

my story ending happily?

Mine did, almost. Grandma said

to Alison, *Some girls grow up*

too fast—you may be one of those—

I didn't see it coming, then

it came. She said, *I promised when*

your mama and your daddy died

I'd never let it, but it did.

I wouldn't say she welcomed me

but said, *A gentleman should walk*

a lady to the door, and rocked

back on her rocking chair, and three

or four a.m.—some mornings, five—

when we came back, rocked in the cold.

I said, *Good morning, Grams*. She said,

Don't push it, boy. Tommy got saved

again. He took a job, fry chef

at Whistle Stop Café, across

from the old cemetery—nowhere

you'd think you'd want to eat though most

folks like the lunch buffet.

Robbery's fun, but when I quit
I didn't miss it much. I'd scored
enough to last till summertime
and Delsym for a hundred years.
March is bleak in Tennessee.
The damp gets in your bones, and though
you know the chill will pass, it throbs.

Alison said she loved me twice
a day, which worried me—since fear
can make a girl announce her love
that way. I kissed her, said, *I love
you too*, a thousand times if one.
She said, *How can you tell?* I said,
*There's many kinds of love—I've got
them all. You make me hard. I feel
that ache like March inside my bones
when we're apart. I want to be
a better man. You need the others?*
Her eyes got wet the way they did,
but happy tears or sad, who knows?
You rest too easy, trouble comes—
the humming and the lullaby

Michael George

and soon the baby's gone, just gone.

She said, *Let's fly*. I hit the gas.

She said, *You see that spot, way out*

in front, where Broad Street turns to dust?

I hit the gas again—again—

but when we got there, there was just

another mile along the road.

She said, *Go—go*. We went and went,

bought tickets at the Tennessee

Safari Park—we saw the llamas,

bison, ostriches, and such—

and when the park closed, Alison

said, *Go—just go and go and go*.

But I turned back to Hollow Rock,

and when I let her out in front,

her eyes were wet—she said, *I wish*

that you weren't such a coward.

8

　　　　When water got inside the wood

and swelled—when bridges iced beneath

my wheels—when phones rang seven times

and no one answered—and Alison

said, *Tommy this and that*—I knew.

First, it's impossible to throw

your gears into reverse when driving

eighty miles a goddamned hour.

Second, love doesn't work that way,

and even if it did. Trying harder

makes it worse, and trying less—

or getting mean or acting like

you don't care what she does or you've

got someone on the side—that makes

it worse than worse. I couldn't see

what she could see in Tommy, which

might be the point. So what I did,

I took her out the way I did

and, when we hit a hundred, punched

it to a hundred ten, and, when

we hit a hundred ten, I gassed

it to a hundred twenty—and

she opened her mouth the way she opened,

and she said, *Wheeeeee*, and I was singing,

It's very clear, our love is here,

and she inched hard against the stick

shift, knee against the shift—I thought

she'd climb onto my lap, a hundred

twenty, pushing at a hundred

thirty miles an hour. That's when

the engine blew.

9

       I wish I could've lighted us

on fire and wish we could've grown old

the way some people do. I went

to Bob's Used Auto Sales—he had

a V-6 I could lift—but when

you're used to eight, you're used to eight,

and crawling's fine for babies, not

for me. On Broad Street, Wilks Used Cars

had a white Silverado truck

with a V-8. He said, *Hard cash.*

Don't try to bargain—I don't much

like doing business with perverts.

I could've broke his neck. I paid

the cash—the last I had from all

the stores I robbed. Without an engine,

what's a boy to do?

       At one a.m.,

an April rain was falling, dark

on dark. I drove to Alison's

and eased into the driveway, headlights

shining through the black on black,

and watched for Alison to run

out through the rain. I'm waiting still,

you understand? The rain is falling,

always will be falling, and

the dark just gets more dark, and if

I live to eighty, ninety, hell,

a hundred, I'll be waiting still.

Oh, Alison, the things we do

for love.

Which is to say, she didn't come.

Grandma said, *Who? Alison?*

She went out half past ten with Tommy.

She winked, like winking made her smart

or was original. I said,

You mean with methhead Tommy? Tick-

tick Tommy, special price for you?

She said, *I mean the one that works*

at Whistle Stop—the one that's got

a job. I could've broke her neck.

I climbed down off that porch, and though

the rain was falling hard and harder,

cold and cold, I didn't feel it,

and Grandma said, *I'm in no rush*

to see you back here anymore.

A girl moves on—it's best you moved

on too. I said, *Grandma, it seems*

like we got off on the wrong foot

a long, long time ago. My love

is true. She said, *I know the song,*

but I don't see the dance. Just what

do you intend for Alison?

I said, *I wish to marry her.*

She said, *You'll have to kill me first.*

I said, *We could arrange that—how's*

next Tuesday?

10

      I drove to Tommy's house.

The lights were on in front, in back,

and in between. The windows shook

with bass beat. April rain pounded

the street. Ten cars—I knew them all

from Uncle's parties—parked along

the side and down in ditches. If

I drove the Silverado up

the lawn, onto the porch, and through

the front wall, who would be surprised?

A bad boy did these things. And so

I did. A truck just ten hours off

the dealer's lot. A V-8 running

low the way a heart does when

it's strong and calm. A tank of gas,

enough to last a day or two.

The splinters flew, like April earth

got sick of rain, fired back at the sky.

There's sounds of thunder, sounds of truck

loads settling on their semi beds,

and sounds of slamming doors you mean

to close real soft, but there ain't none

like Silverados ramming up

the steps and crashing through the siding,

two-by-fours, and drywall, crushing

everything. That sound is like

God spoke.

      And when God speaks, a freckled

girl you met at Uncle's lies

in a sad heap, her elbow bent

this way, that way, a smile still pasted

from words she heard before the wall

came down—I hoped she wasn't dead—

smoke hanging in the smoky light,

                —and savage faces

poking from doorways like in some

old flick—then Tommy in underpants

yelled, *What the fuck?* and *What the fuck?*

I climbed down from my truck, inspected

how much damage. Some boys like

their Fords, some GMCs, but if

you want to drive up Tommy's front

porch, through the wall, and half across

the living room, I recommend

a Chevy. Sure, a chunk of two-by-four stuck sideways from the grill—

they make the front ends soft to take

the blow—and pride but only pride

and not necessity would cost

another thousand bucks before

I got it right. Then Tommy spun

his fists—a bad mistake. I yanked

the chunk of wood out of the grill

and mashed his teeth, and my-oh-my,

what years of smoke and snorting didn't,

a two-by-four did, down and down,

teeth snowing on the rug. Then Tommy's

uncle had a kitchen knife—

I danced with him a little, watching

how he swung, then moved in fast

and wrecked his face. He sliced my shoulder—

I credit him—most wasted junkies

too damn slow. Then Tommy's friends—

the boyfriend of the girl whose arm

I broke—came out with lamps and fists

and forks and, one of them, a toaster—

I broke the toaster on his head

and asked the others, *Do you want*

to fight a boy whose only sin

is that he loves too much? They did.

When they went down, another came

from the garage, a hammer in

his hand. I felt real tired, like ain't

enough enough? I said, *Just give*

me Alison. She's all I came for.

He said, *You see this hammer?—It's*

the only lips you'll kiss tonight.

I said, *You make me want to cry.*

I don't know who'd have died, that boy

or me, one surely—he was angry,

and I was tired of angry boys

with tools too heavy for their arms.

He swung the hammer, and I grabbed

his throat—then Alison—her shirt

unbuttoned, her pink high-top sneakers

loose, unlaced—she seemed to drift

in like a ghost—I thought she was dead,

I thought a moment I was too,

and Tommy's house, the splintered light,

a railroad car, riding the tracks

of Hollow Rock Branch heavenward

to hell. I let the hammer boy

go then—he backed off like he saw

it too—I said, *Hey, girl.* She looked

at me like mud. I let her take

it in—the girl with the bent arm

and Tommy with no teeth and Tommy's

uncle with a board-sized mash

right where his nose should be. I said,

I'll slaughter armies, Alison.

      She looked at me like I

was long ago. *We're leaving now,*

I said. She said, *You had your chance.*

I said, *You ain't no lottery ticket—*

And me? I ain't a boy put down.

She touched the girl whose arm I broke

and said, *I'm sorry,* shed a tear

for Tommy's uncle, got down on her knees

and picked up teeth like they were seashells.

Baby, she said to Tommy, *Baby—*

and that was it for me, that word

of tenderness—no tears—she took

the world in white enamel pieces—

she held it in her hand, and squeezed.

She stared at me, her eyes as hard

as teeth, and said, *You'd best be leaving.*

I took her wrist—the hand that held

the teeth—I would've crushed her had

she not let go—and all those pieces

snowed back to earth where they belonged

till summer came. The look she gave

me—was it love or hate? It was.

I said, *Your bones are mine. My bones*

are yours. She tried to take her hand

back, but her hand was mine—I said,

Skin, blood, and muscle, yours and mine.

She said, *It's time you left*. I said,

Your bones, my bones, our bones. I dragged

her to the truck. She didn't scream.

She didn't cry. She seemed a root

in old clay soil—a stone embedded

in earth—but times a boy becomes

a man if only for a while,

his one hand like an avalanche,

his other dangling keys as light

as butterflies. I put her in

the truck beside me, raced the engine,

clouded up the room with fumes,

and shifted to Reverse. You can't

turn time, and dust and smoke will hang

Michael George

in clouds for weeks and months. I touched

the pedal, and the pickup rolled

right out across the porch and down

the steps—the April night rain pounding

the hood and windshield, blinding me

to all the damage I had done.

I said, *Hold tight now, Alison*—

You always said you want to see

the moon.

I found the driveway, found the road.

She tried to bail out where Old Pisgah

turns to Seminary, but

I thumbed the power lock and said,

No, honey, no. Between United

Methodist and Cherry Creek

she got her window halfway down—

I locked it too. She clawed and clawed

me with her fingernails, screamed Bastard,

but I said, *Babe, I love your touch.*

She raked me bloody till we hit

the Hollow Rock Branch crossing, and

we flew like a jet fighter till

we didn't and she cracked her head

against the Silverado roof—

that calmed her down a breath or two.

She said, *I hate you*, which is what

a girl says when she loves you and

you've made her mad, but also when

she hates you real—so how's a boy

to know? At Broad Street, I said, *East*

or west? She said, *You asshole*, which

I figured might mean east, so I

turned west. I said, *You ever think*

of California? Ever dream

of desert skies? She said, *I've got*

the sheriff's number, and I said,

You ever think of roads without

a light to stop you when you go?

She said, *I gotta pee*. I said,

It took me all these years of going

nowhere but I understand—

I swear I do.

The April rain

came hard and harder—wipers wiping

dark and darker—fifteen minutes

out to Huntington, another

twenty down to Cedar Grove—

I-40, where Love's Travel Stop

was beating like a neon heart.

She said, *I really gotta pee.*

I said, *You'll wait till Arkansas.*

She said, *The toilets better there?*

I said, *I mean to show you I*

can leave. She tried to bail again

on the I-40 ramp—I held

the lock and said, *You may be cute*

but you ain't smart.

                    A hundred miles

to Memphis and I wasn't faking

anymore. I know that what

I did was wrong—but if I lost

an inch each time, I'd be a hole

so deep. I know I should've turned

back home and said, *I'm sorry, so,*

so sorry—but I wasn't sorry

and felt a little dizzy from

the fighting and the dark and rain.

No, Alison,

I said, *if loving you is wrong—*

then sang it like they used to do.

She said, *I really really gotta.*

The Memphis lights, like flaming tears,

like city streets and skies could cry

the way she did behind the stands—

seemed half a life ago—shined acid—

the dark so dark until the streaks

like clawing fingernails down faces—

I got real quiet. I slowed, and her

wide eyes got wider, like, you know,

she'd never seen such beauty—falling

stars on summers nights, drumming

the earth and burning where they struck.

I said, *It's something, right?* She laughed,

and for a moment, I believed

we'd come at last to where we had

been going.

Around the bend, and the Hernando

de Soto Bridge, which reached across

the Mississippi River, rose,

two humps of steel, strung up in lights—

I said, *Right? Right?*

        Then, Arkansas—

West Memphis—flat and dull and wet

as Mississippi River floods—

stretched out beyond the bridge, how many

miles of dark and deeper dark—

and Alison no longer laughed.

I tried—I grinned and said, *Right* once

again, but there was no denying

that Arkansas was wrong.

11

She said, *I gotta pee.* I said,

For God's sake then. Five miles beyond

the farther bank, another truck

stop—Flying J—the kind of place

whores sleep beneath the eighteen-wheelers

on rainy April nights if no

one's buying, go inside the stop

for Denny's pancakes if they are.

I parked along the semi-trucks

because, well, hell, a truck's a truck.

I gave my lecture. *Alison,*

I trust you—Alison, this world

is nothing without us in it—

look 'round, and all you see is night

except for us.

        I touched the lock—

just touched it—and she touched the handle

like it might've been a trick.

The door swung open—and she stopped.

She turned and kissed me on the lips.

Then she was gone—like black wind sucked

her from the pickup, gone—you hear

those stories of an airplane when

an exit door blows out, the way

the sky sucks out the inside—see

it in a movie or a nightmare—

the slick night's hungry for a body,

and when the body's gone it never

comes back, never. Alison

was gone—and one pink high-top sneaker

lying on the pickup floor,

the other tumbling out into

the night—and I yelled, *Alison,*

the way in movies and in nightmares—

your voice is gone, because a ghost

or something worse has stolen it.

I watched the black night, listened to

the voice I didn't have.

                              She went

and went—I couldn't say how far—

I tumbled out and followed her

across the truck stop lot—but she

was gone, was running barefoot like

the asphalt turned to meadow, like

a rainy night in summer, running

so fast, I never saw a girl

run quite so fast.

She seemed to know

where she was going—how could she

have known?—a semi-truck cab, throbbing,

the trailer a black tongue—and how

could she have known the door would open

like a mouth, a hand reach out

to help her up and in, the way

some animals run out onto

a road, desiring death, it seems,

or mutilation?

I stopped. I stood

and took the rain, which felt like ice.

The semi-truck cab throbbed and throbbed—

I thought my heart had stopped. I stood

and watched. The truck rolled from its spot

and seemed to know what it was doing.

I stood—the sky was falling like

the rain—if nothing else survived,

that semi-truck would—I was cold

and would've stood forever like

a stone, but felt eyes watching from

another truck, an all-pink cab—

a woman trucker staring like

I'd sinned. And so I had. I slunk

back to my pickup, broken souled,

and fired the engine, drove and drove

and drove. What was a boy to do

but drive?

THE CHAPLAIN

1

We're transdenominational—

we love you as you are and were

and will be.

Jesus knew that sinners make

the best apostles—prostitutes

and addicts, thieves and angry men

who fight with other men and God.

These are our congregants or we

have none. You sleep with wolves and eat

with vultures? We've a home for you.

You bathe in tar? We shall not judge you,

brother. We've consorted with

far worse. Drink from the cup—it will

refresh you.

We've Jerry on electric. He

was once a beaner, driving strung-

out forty-eight or sixty hours

without a break for sleep or prayer.

He testified the things he did,

and now he sings in praise of God

and plays guitar, sowing the seeds

of gospel. Debbie, on the drums—

would you believe she turned three tricks

an hour before the hepatitis?—

another sinner Jesus saved.

And me? My mama was

a gravedigger. My daddy was

a fist. I ran away at sixteen,

enlisted at eighteen, spent time

in prison for a robbery

I didn't do, and then I drove

for fifteen years before I found

the Lord. Our tent is longer than

the road and wider than the sky.

You know there's plenty room for you.

In truth I've had some trouble with

the lesbians and fags. I've prayed

to God for better understanding.

Jews and Blacks I tolerate

and even love. If God can do

that for a man like me, believe

he'll do it for you too.

As members of

Christ's body, Christian souls, we owe

it to each other and ourselves

to try our best to love. I can't

absolve you of the harm you've done—

that's the Lord's work. I'll cry with you

or hold your hand and listen while

you do. I never met a man

who didn't seek a better way.

We raised our tent outside

the Flying J—West Memphis draws

in sinners by the horde. I told

my sermon to the prostitutes

who wandered in to shelter from

the sun. I told the parable

of Balaam's lazy ass from Numbers,

twenty-two—

                 Balaam played

chicken with an angel of

the Lord on a forsaken Utah

highway, high-beams blinding in

the dark. He shifted gears and hit

the gas, determined he would die

before he'd yield. The two trucks bore

down on each other—glory in

the night—and Balaam swore he'd end

this trip in fire. But in his hands

the wheel turned of its own against

his fearsome grip. His truck slid to

the side.

   In Napa Valley some

time later, in among the vineyards,

Balaam hauled ammonium nitrate

to fertilize the grapes.

The Lord put on a dress—a tiny

thing, with lovely legs—and stood

along the roadside with a thumb—

and Balaam stopped, as truckers will

for lovely legs. She climbed into

his truck cab, stuck a pistol in

his ribs, and stole his wallet, left

him broke and scared.

    Then Balaam, with

a load of Samsung flat-screens for

a Cincinnati Best Buy, stopped

in Dayton where a buddy wanted

one. Outside an alley on

the eastside of the city, God

admonished Balaam with the law.

As Balaam slept that night in jail,

the Lord spoke to him—*I've come here,*

opposing you, because your path's

a reckless one. And in that vision,

Balaam found his way.

Now, brother, since that night, I've preached

along the roadsides, Debbie on

the drums and Jerry on guitar.

Apostles travel where the angels

point them—ask Paul, who was Saul—

but mostly through the southern states.

Apostles open up their souls—

they emanate the light that shines

within. They never hide their lamps

in baskets—Matthew tells us, *Let*

your light so shine that all may see.

      I've met some troubled men,

some troubled women—lost, as I

was lost. I've prayed and cried and cried

and prayed, and some have said my tears

and prayers consoled them.

2

                    Mrs. Traney,

who taught sophomore history

at Valley Christian High School, told us,

Time and space are absolute.

She made her point before they fired

her for her tiny dress and lovely

legs. She said, in India

a Hindu Brahma year is like

three trillion human years, which blew

my sixteen-year-old mind. For them,

space comes three flavors—physical

and psychological and, third,

a space of consciousness, this last

one infinite, which means you'd better

charge by the mile, not the whole journey.

That's a Hindu trucker joke.

She taught about the Aztecs too.

They thought time went in circles, which

the ancient Chinese also thought.

The Aztecs didn't separate

their sense of space from sense of time,

so every highway came to where

Michael George

it started, which made driving hard,

deliveries confusing, brother.

For Eskimos, she told us, time

and space are *fundamentally*

unstable—fundamentally—

though no one much cares what they think.

The point is Christianity's

the only faith for truckers—with

the alpha and omega, the

beginnings, middles, ends. I tried

my hardest with Mrs. Traney, asked

her for the extra lessons, this

before Christ saved me. Sure, a tiny

dress and lovely legs are sweet

as Sunday music. Boys are boys,

and men are men. We might forgive

ourselves for what we've done, since God does.

                  I don't believe

in holding boys accountable

for what they do before they're grown.

If all the sixteen-year-olds died

and went to hell, they'd bugger Satan—

that's the way God made them.

Mrs. Traney told

me, *Don't*, and then she told me, *Do*.

She seemed as mixed up as I was.

They fired her and suspended me

eight weeks. I never went back after—

sixteen years enough to know

I'd had enough. I saw her at

the Aldi with her husband—I

said, *Hey*—and then I learned the way

the guy from Deuteronomy

who violates his neighbor's wife

felt when the neighbors gathered stones.

I left Mom's eggs in aisle three

and sprinted for the exit. Men

in Tennessee have guns or they

aren't men, and Mr. Traney was

a man with bullets in his eyes.

Brother,

you understand, like Augustine,

I danced in fire before I bathed

in Jesus's blood. I hang my head

but say that without shame.

3

                    Long

before I drove into West Memphis,

I smelled the rot of Ten Mile Bayou,

felt the tractor-trailers rumbling,

heard the ringing slot machines.

I had a vision of a black-

tongued man. He drove a Freightliner

Cascadia, a DD16

engine under the hood, a cab

with space enough to love a woman.

I saw him in my vision steaming—

he'd take a mile to stop, so heavy

and terrible his load. I saw

him tearing through black wastes, the farmlands

broken still before spring planting

as Edom's streams shall turn to pitch.

Brother, I seldom suffer visions.

When I do, I write them in

a book I hope to publish one

day soon, the testimony of

my time abroad. My motto is

Pray boldly and pray often. Yield

yourself. And so I traveled to

West Memphis where my vision said

to go. I raised my tent and sang

my songs. Between Mark One, which says,

And rising early in the morning,

while it was still dark, he went

out to a desolate place and prayed,

and what I call the trucker's Psalm—

The Lord's my strength and shield—I asked

the congregants to testify.

      A broken prostitute

named Tra—which is a lovely name,

I said, and sang it, *Tra-la-la*—

she told a story we've all heard

too many times, of bottoming out

till Jesus found her in the swill,

a needle in her arm. I raised

my hands—and voice—and said, *God bless*

you, sister, which is how I tell

them they can sit back down. But she

kept tra-la-la-ing till I signaled

Debbie and she started up

on drums.

A Denny's line cook stood and spoke,

a torn-up man if ever the world

tore men. A prisoner half his life,

he lived now with his sister's son.

The steel of time had scraped him raw,

and all he had was faith, a dollar

more than minimum wage, and all

the coffee he could drink for free.

He said he was a sinner through

and through, and he began to cry.

I said, *I love you, brother—Jesus*

loves you too—and tears will wash

you to the shore of Galilee.

                    Then Jerry played

the riff from Kid Rock's "Trucker Anthem."

Debbie passed the plate. I said,

The Lord's my strength and shield. My heart

exults, and—

                              Back

behind the cooler which we filled

with Gatorade for days the tent

got overheated with God's work,

a trucker in a trucker's hat

cleared his throat, said, *Preacher, I've*

had conversations with your God,

and I've concluded you and he

are frauds.

          I laughed. *Them's fighting words,*

I said, the way the cartoons say

it, *and the good Lord loves a fight.*

With all the weapons in this world,

it's best to save them with a smile,

but back down neither.

              The trucker threw

his hat down—oily black hair snaking—

and came at me the way a man

don't come to take the wine and wafer.

He said, *I hate a fraud, can't stand*

a hypocrite.

          I knew I'd meet

that sort of man, and Debbie knew

it too. She had a .22

inside a bag she kept behind

the bass drum—went for it, like fire.

The trucker fixed her with his stare.

I swear the pistol seemed to melt

in Debbie's hand. He told the others,

Scat—like they were rodents. No

one moved—for fear, and not for courage.

He left. I followed him outside.

He crossed the lot and disappeared

into his long black Freightliner.

      I felt the fear too, brother—

felt the fear a man feels facing

evil along the highway in

West Memphis. But before I went

inside the tent to salvage what

I could, I saw another sight,

which eased my soul. A lady driver

stepped outside the Flying J

convenience store in white jeans and

black leather, feathered blonde hair, looking

like an angel. She held—I swear—

one little pink shoe. She carried it

the way she might a chalice. Stunned—

she looked real stunned—as if she moved

against a holy light. There was

no wind that morning in mid-May,

and yet, I felt it blow, enough

to cleanse the land.

Michael George

4

   The first time Debbie came

to me, outside Augusta, near

to Hancock Landing, where we'd parked

by the Savannah River—Jerry

gone to Thomson to check out

the truck stop there—and she'd been drinking—

maybe I'd been too—and what

I'm saying, brother—trying to say—

is I have been a hypocrite.

That man spoke truth. I don't believe

hypocrisy is quite the same

as fraud. I understand you may

and others might. But when a woman

smells like wine, ambassadors

of God get lonely too. The road

to heaven's long—we stop to rest.

   The women I

like most are soft. Debbie is hard,

a human elbow, skin years under

the desert sand, her eyes as small

and hard as knuckles, but her breath

as sweet as wine.

        She took her shirt off, gazed

at me. A cup of dice that shakes

and spills, and when the dice go still,

the other possibilities—

the eights or fives that could've been

but weren't—all disappear and seem

like numbers God himself despises.

That's how I saw her eyes and knew

what the number meant for her,

for me.

        I told her, *Draw*

me after you. Let us make haste,

for I am sick with love.

        She took

me through the forest by the river.

Our couch was green, our rafters pine.

I said, *Stay with me now.*

        Her fingers,

a trigger squeezing, she said, *Do*

me, Preacher, till I beg for mercy.

I gave her what she asked for, gave

her all I had.

Michael George

And afterward

we bathed together in the river,

loved and bathed.

              Then Jerry came

and, standing on the bank, bewildered,

told us the Savannah was

the third most toxic river in

America. He'd read it and

believed it true. The hand of God

was on us—Debbie knew it and

I knew.

              From that day forth,

we loved in sadness and in shame.

I tell you so you know—I've been

a sinner too.

5

West Memphis turned

a bounty. Men and women came

from miles around, the crippled and

the spiritually lame. In towns

like Edmondson and Crawfordsville,

there's hunger for new voices that

aren't neighbors, hens, or cows. I had

a voice, and Jerry played guitar,

and Debbie—bless her loving heart—

had rhythm.

They came—

a cockeyed boy on bicycle,

a lady with a stutter and

two friends, a putrid man no one

could bear to sit near till the other

chairs were full. The ministers—

from Ebenezer Church, First Baptist,

Zion Field, New Bethel—left

their flocks to graze without them, came

and muttered in the back as Debbie

drummed the pulse of our salvation.

Michael George

A man set up a barbeque.

The *Evening Times* sent out a kid

to get the story. When it ran,

the seventh day, our tent near split

its threads. We lifted high above

the Flying J. We prayed and praised

and sang—and slept but little.

      When the trucker in

the Freightliner Cascadia

came back, I hardly recognized him.

He'd shaved his hair off, bald head shining

pale as daylight, mirrored glasses

glinting, like a man who wished

to terrorize from thick inside

the crowd or wanted to be seen

but unacknowledged.

      I did

my *Rising early in the morning*

part and called upon the folk

to testify. The stuttering lady—

who'd tried every morning since

the third without success—stood up

to try again, but back behind

the cooler, the man spoke—*If you*
will not wake up, I'll come like a thief—
you will not know what hour I'll come
against you.

      The cockeyed boy said, *Say it,*
mister. Then the stuttering lady
spoke without a stutter, *Yea,*
if we claim fellowship with him
while walking in the dark, we lie
and do not practice truth.

        A blessing, sure,
I said, and Debbie added, *Praise*
the Lord, and I eyed Jerry, who
riffed "Trucker Anthem." I said, *Next—*
because when congregants start quoting
verses, that's my job, not theirs.
The trucker hadn't finished—said,
He who confesses and forsakes
his sins will obtain mercy, but
he who withholds forgiveness, none—
and all the others turned their ears.
I said, *My friend, what sins have you*
committed? What forgiveness do
you seek?

         Michael George

He grinned and said, *I killed*

a girl.

        The stuttering lady looked

to me as if I'd have a verse

for that, the cockeyed boy laughed like

somebody finally outsmarted

God, and Debbie dropped her drumsticks.

He said, *I killed a girl, and if*

you've faith enough, you'll save my soul.

He eyed me like he'd burn a hole—

A runaway, he said, *she climbed*

into my arms. I buried her

with all the rites that were her due.

If mercy comes from penance, he'd

have none. *I've been a doubter, preacher.*

still I doubt. But if you've got

the power you'll ease my burden.

                    I said,

That's God's work, driver—His, not mine.

But I will pray for you and your

redemption.

        Don't you Goddamned dare,

he said, and went, leaving me speechless

in my tent.

6

For three days then, the tent was empty.

Jerry said, *The rain*. It's true—

the rain came heavy for three days.

There's time enough for Jesus, said

the line cook when he brought our lunch.

But if the highway system was

a story, the twists and turns would tangle

beginnings, middles, ends—and when

would time enough be time enough?

In those three days, I wondered if

West Memphis was the end—my end—

of every story, every road.

The fourth day, when the rain stopped, Jerry

played guitar—Metallica

and Aerosmith and Korn—and Debbie

gazed at me the way she did

before she stripped her shirt off. Brother,

I felt temptation too. A man's

a man. The first mistake is thinking

otherwise, and then pride swells,

and when pride swells, we're damned in heaven,

Michael George

damned on earth, for all the proud

and lofty shall be humbled.

I went to Debbie, took

her. Jerry closed his eyes and played

a dirty lick.

Who knows what hell we would've

harrowed but the cockeyed boy

ducked underneath a tent flap, fell

into a chair—a grin like he'd

been drinking whiskey in the rain—

and said, *God save America*,

which must've meant a thing to him.

Then Tra the prostitute came back

and sat by him. And soon, the line

cook joined them on the side.

That day,

we held a service for those three,

but two days later seven came,

counting the largest man I've ever

seen, a giant in overalls.

He had the sweetest singing voice

when singing hymns.

                    Around that time,

state troopers stopped and talked to drivers

driving through. A preacher has

responsibilities to God

foremost and secondarily

to people, owes the state no debt

at all except when governments

and holy law align. What did

I know? The words an angry man

spoke. When a trooper asked, I held

my tongue.

I've seen injustice, suffered it,

won't tolerate it when I can

oppose it. Prisoners I called

my friends at Otter Creek took beatings

like unbeaten men. I took

the beatings too, unearned or earned.

I know what Mr. Fischer did

to Cindy when he caught us in

his warehouse—we were kids, just kids.

I know how Cindy never got

right after. When she cut herself,

they rolled their eyes and said, *That Goddamned*

Cindy. When a rockslide crushes

cars in Chattanooga or

the French Broad River floods and drowns

a child, they bow their heads and say,

God's will be done. Not me—I doubt

my faith at times. I won't condemn

another man. If that's a form

of cowardice, then call me coward.

7

A coward, but I'd have you know
what sort I am.

      I ran away at sixteen,
spent my forty desert days
alone the way a boy must, ate
from garbage, came to Nashville where
there sang around me in my ears
a cauldron of unholy loves.
I lived with vermin, walked a mile
in others' shoes, which, I admit,
I stole. I met my best friend, Crazy
Tim. We lit the city streets
on fire and beat up alcoholics,
drank their booze. At seventeen,
I fought death's angel at St. Thomas
Midtown Hospital when Crazy
Tim's shank cost me half my spleen.
The cops said, *Son, can you explain*
what happened to the other boy?
I said, *I can't.* They gave me choices—
seldom do we get them on

         Michael George

this road—enlist or face the charges.

Uniforms fit tight on boys,

but prison bars fit tighter, so

I signed and cooked the next two years

at Fort McNair—fried eggs for breakfast,

beans for lunch and dinner.

           Dishonor's in

the eye of the beholder, Jesus's

love is absolute, and that's

the difference. The army had

its rules as armies do. On base,

a soldier walks on pavement, not

on grass, and feeds the men the army

tells him to. Supply room rules

prohibit theft for any reason,

even helping dancers from

the Good Guys Club pay rent.

The army tolerates the evil

spirits and infirmities

of men on fighting fields, but stateside

do your duty or go home.

They sent me home. I shared a two-
room with a car thief named Maurice
at Wedgewood West Apartments out
in Annandale. It's funny how
God works, though at that time I didn't
laugh. We drove to Lottie's Liquors
to celebrate my freedom. While
I waited outside in a stolen
Nissan Sport, Maurice shot both
the cashiers in the gut and danced
out with a bottle in each hand.
I told the judge I didn't do it
and didn't know he would.
She sentenced me to ten years—I
served six and change. My goodness, I
was mangy when they turned the key.

My story's true,
as all salvations are, though names
and details change to suit the crowd.
I drove for J.B. Hunt ten years
and Schneider National for five,
and now I spread good news from town
to town. I don't pretend to be

a better man than I have been.

I'd sooner have you soak my boots

in spit than bathe my feet.

8

We left

West Memphis on a rainy morning.

May was come, and Debbie felt

the urge to drive. We drifted north

that summer, spent some heated days

in Kansas City and St. Louis.

I baptized three in the Missouri

River, three the Mississippi,

one the Carlyle Reservoir.

In Warrenton, we set up shop

outside another Flying J,

and when the nights got hot we rented

rooms, and in the afternoons—

when truckers fixed their eyes down highways

miles and miles before the dark

and rarely gazed at God or heaven—

Debbie and I found a spot

in Little Lost Creek Conservation

where we could be all alone

and never speak of innocence

or guilt. We found that spot and lived

a while each afternoon the way

I'd never lived before and maybe

never will again. I've heard

folks say of other times and places,

Life was sweet, and guessed that they

were telling lies or fooling with

their memories, but in the black

oak shade, our life was sweet—the wild

grass odor in the heat. I know

we've fallen, know God's gravity

works just the same as earth's, and once

you're down you don't get up until

the Judgment Day. I know beginnings,

middles, ends. I know the garden

smell of wild grass, weeds, and summer

soil is only an illusion,

know it in my mind and sometimes

my heart. But on those afternoons,

our life was sweet.

We found no welcome when we drove

to Springfield, raised our praising tent

outside the Auburn Travel Center.

a man who didn't like guitar

fought Jerry with his fists and knife—

which Jerry won but got nine stitches.

He said he now would answer to

the name of Israel, though I told

him Jacob never played "Free Bird,"

and, if he did, God never minded.

At Kennett Truck Stop—just a mile

from the Ohio River on

the Indiana side—Elvis,

photographed in black and white,

sang out from every wall—and, in

a case, a dial telephone

that never rang, old radios

that never played, and, at the counter,

oyster crackers if you ordered

chili. Debbie said it was

the sort of place she'd always sought for,

talked of staying put a year

or two, but then she got a cramp—

could be from too much happiness—

and so we broke the tent and kept

our pilgrimage.

While driving from that place

back to Kentucky—two a.m.

or maybe three—I had another

vision, bad to have when roads

are slick and black with summer rain,

but when a vision strikes, a man

must see—

A pink-cab truck, bobtailing

like it dropped a demon load

and meant to run before the earth

boiled over, came around a bend

near Sadieville, its headlights flashing

like a glory in the night,

and, when we passed—this way and that—

the lady driver was the same

who carried a pink shoe the way

she might a chalice from the store

at Flying J some months before.

I said, *Praise be,* though Debbie slept

beside me and if Jerry heard

he didn't say, but when the sun

rose three hours later we drove back

through Tennessee, breathing the fumes

like Jesus's disciples.

9

We caught up when

she pulled off outside Gordonsville,

a dozen little posters in

her hand. Said, *HAVE YOU SEEN THIS GIRL?*—

a picture of a kid who looked

like trouble of a sort I know

too well. You see it in the teeth—

and she was smiling, as a troubled

kid does till she learns to hide

the signs. The lady driver taped

her posters to the poles, and as

I watched I dreamed the words I still

dream after all these pilgrim years—

That's Cindy, Goddamned Cindy—and

I felt I the pang I always feel.

I asked

the driver, *Who's this Alison*

to you?

She seemed to know the sort

of man who asked such things. She said,

The girl's a ghost who haunts these roads.

Do you believe in ghosts?

                    I said,

The Holy Ghost, the Father, and

the Son.

      She eyed me then and said,

Oh, you're that one.

               I said, *You know me?*

That made her laugh. She said, *A nomad*

living in a goat-hair tent

and telling lies and stealing silver

from passersby.

          I said, *They give*

me copper mostly, if I get

a coin at all. There are worse ways

to make dishonest livings. What's

your con? The girl your kid or is

she anyone's?

             I tell you, brother,

I've known some women who will cut

a man with broken glass. I've known

some with thick shoulders, some who breathe

invective, burning ears to cinders.

Others hold their anger in

their chests—those ones the kind who stared

down Nero's lions.

                    In the dawn

of central Tennessee, the lady

seemed to wonder which she was,

then said, *I've driven thirty thousand*

miles in search of something I

can't name, although I know they call

her Alison—a sense of when

I was a child of six, before

a boy named Jimmy Acorn took

me back behind the house, a sense

of something like a knot of dirty

twine I carried in my pocket,

more valuable to me than gold

or love, though it might be the same

as love.

10

For thirteen days, we followed her
from stop to stop. We pasted posters
on pumps and walls. We asked the drivers
whether they'd seen a barefoot girl
who looked like Alison, a black-
tongued man, or both. We stowed the tent
and hymnals—There's a time to speak,
a time for silence, time to rend
or sew. No one acknowledged seeing
Alison and when we asked
about a man with oily hair,
or bald, and wicked eyes he hid
with mirrored shades, the drivers shook
their heads and walked away.

We went to Denver, went
to Rapid City, went to Dallas,
zigzagged back to Louisville,
and learned the gnawing feel when absence
meets desire.
                    Debbie drummed
her drumsticks on the dashboard, looking

more pissed off with every mile.

She said, *I didn't sign up for*

this voyage.

Jerry sat in back,

his face as blank as pavement when

he said, *How long before we get*

there?

A Sunday morning—we were in

Fort Wayne—I told the lady, *There's*

a time.

She slapped a poster on

a trashcan, said, *Give me that tape.*

I said, *A time to every purpose*

under heaven.

The other tape,

she said.

I said, *A time to hate,*

a time of war, a time of stones,

a time to kill.

She smoothed and smoothed

the poster on the can and said,

Spit it out, Preacher.

I said, *A time*

to go back home.

Michael George

And so we drove

back to West Memphis where there sang

around us in a cauldron sounds

of crying children.

11

We raised the tent

and spoke of peace and watched the sky

for signs, and off-ramps for a black-

tongued man.

The cockeyed boy returned

and brought his sister.

The Denny's line

cook told us Tra was at St. Jude's,

tuberculosis ripping up

her lungs, and, though we couldn't visit,

we prayed.

August turned September, and

the first October nights were cool

and cold. Then Debbie said New Orleans

called. Last time I saw her, all

I saw was thumb.

The lady driver

lived on Red Bull, Stimamine,

and biscuits—jittered like she meant

to dance when Jerry played guitar

and, when he stopped, seemed like a pain

was gouging her inside. I looked

to her when calling for the lost

to rise and testify, but she

kept counsel with herself. I said,

God loves you, sister, and I passed

the cup, but sometimes running dry's

the only way to run.

                    When Jerry

talked of Texas, I thought my work

was done. Was time to break the tent

and go. I would've gone, except

that afternoon a slick, black truck

came down the exit from I-40,

rolled along the service road

as if time had no middle and

no end—the driver born at the

creation, living there still, all

the world before him—parked behind

the tent and cast us in his shade.

The man climbed out, his mirrored glasses

perched on his head, grinning a grin

that said he'd heard it all before.

                He stood behind

the cooler, the lady driver to

his side. He wore a lumber jacket,

jeans, and leather boots, and looked

like he'd been living well.

                        I said, *God bless*

you, friend. We've waited days and days

for you. What would you drink? What eat?

What solace can we offer a man

like you?

          He grinned that black-tongued grin,

and said, *The joke's on you,* and for

a time I thought he'd pull a gun.

I told him, *If you've come to speak,*

we'll listen—if you wish to sing

and pray, we'll sing and pray with you—

but if you've filled your coat with coal,

you'll kindly step outside and let

us breathe.

          He said, *Too late for you*

to beg forgiveness—absolution's

a lie—as if he was the preacher

and I the suffering reprobate.

The lady driver stood and faced him,

a mountain where she'd trembled. *Come*

                                                                   Michael George

with me, she said—that's all.

He put

his glasses on. The mirrored lenses

seemed to help him see. She took

his hand as if she'd guide a child,

and said, *Oh, come with me*. She could've

sung, she wanted him so bad.

I'll show you why you've come so far.

He went—a child who'd found

a rusty blade—as if he'd found

the prize he'd sought.

They crossed

the parking lot to where her truck

was, crossed—I stood outside the tent

and watched. They opened up and climbed

inside.

I've gone

to Babylon in dreams and heard

the seven-headed beast rise up

and roar its blasphemy, and, brother,

what I heard as her truck pulled

across the lot and rolled along

the service road was such a roar.

LADY DRIVER

1

Driver, you're hammer down,

hauling across the sands of time—

heat worms turning, dying on

the asphalt in the sun. You have

a thousand miles before you sleep.

You're popping beans until your head's

a microwave turned high and set

to eternity.

I have a little girl myself.

We've all been there, no use you crying.

Driver, when you think of it,

a salty tear hits desert sand

like bacon blood hits skillet—gone,

just gone, and all that's left is flesh

and fat, which is the way of things.

You're nothing to the mountains, nothing

to God. Your tears roll down and if

they don't roll down to the plains, they rinse

in mountain streams until the salt

is gone. If anything remains

no one will see to know. No, when

your salt is gone, your salt is gone.

What I'm saying is women don't

need to be ragged at because we are

truck drivers. You said, *You're too damn pretty*

for a truck driver, and I could've

opened the door and let you out.

Driver,

it ain't the way it used to be.

Not like I eat my pumpkin pie

on Christmas Day—no, there's a season

for everything, a time and place.

There we were and here we are,

and what use blaming, with miles and miles

of road between? What use excuses?—

your mama's drinking, my daddy's belt,

your auntie, my brother, your teacher, my preacher,

Jimmy Acorn behind the house,

me six years old. The point is, driver,

no use blaming. What doctor's note

has saved a man from standing in

the firing line? What *so sorry*

ever turned him back as he

went out the door?

Plain and simple, it ain't worth it.

Why fight? These chains are good for more

than snow and ice. If eighty thousand

pounds of Class 8 wheel and steel

don't break them, why do you think you will?

The hardest chains are in your head.

When I rattle yours, know what

I hear? A young girl screaming.

                              The way

folks put their ears to rails and say,

Train's coming, train's surely coming—

Kentucky caverns, you whisper at

one end, your friend, a mile through twist

and turn, hears clear as wind is how

I hear that girl.

                    Some truck stops clean,

some filthy. Mama's cooking?—those

are the exceptions. Some are safe

and some Godawful frightening, none

more so than where *you* fill your tanks,

driver, shower for your dime,

and play the slots. Sound travels faster

through solid than air. I hear her calling

still through asphalt and steel. You thought

cramming an oil rag in her mouth

would quiet her. It never works

that way. It's just a shifting load.

Oversized don't always mean

overweight. Ain't worth it—often

it ain't.

My daddy was a driver, said

I didn't need to look like ass

just because I drove a truck.

I said, *Daddy, I ain't about*

to shame myself—and I got out

of there soon as my toes grew long

enough to reach the floor. He said,

The life ain't worth it—lived it three

weeks out, two days at home, and knew

the costs and benefits. He said,

Baby, it ain't the life for you,

which meant, it was the life for me.

I tell you this because there is

a point to it. The point is, I

learn slow but learn. If nothing else

about the trucking life, there's time

to learn—there's time and miles—and when

I heard her cry, I thought, *Now, who's*

that singing? The singing went like that

for weeks, me none the wiser, like

rumors you hear while thinking about

more rumors, and it's only later

you properly can hear them. You wake

inside your cab—sucking your thumb—

say, *Damn*, because you fairly heard it—

a screaming girl, pretty as pink.

Some truck drivers, they blow smoke,

talk shit. I got two words for them.

Carbon monoxide. Sooner or later,

Carbon monoxide. Some of them

the shotgun if it gets too late,

they get too tired, but most of them

the slow C.O. That's after miles

and miles, and never thinking, *Open*

the windows, dumbass. Dying's slow

like that but it ain't easy. Maybe

it takes ten years or more, but comes—

a hundred thousand miles a year

it comes, across the deserts, mountains,

grassy plains.

I'd get you water, driver, but there's

no water. Wine, but there's no wine.

I do not wish to ease your soul.

2

The girl grew up in Hollow Rock.

Once had a general store until

God said, *Hasta la vista, baby*,

and rats ate the last box of oats.

The kind of place you're always leaving.

The girl grew up,

The girl got out, her grandma told me,

rocking. *Was a boy she fell for.*

Always a boy and always falling,

my Alison. Her name—you know it,

driver, in the skin you know

her name was Alison.

No use denying, driver, no

use trying to spit out the rag,

and no use trying to split chains—

you ain't King Kong, you ain't a horse—

you ain't even a real man.

Listen, driver. Listen hard.

In Utah there's a single tree

called Trembling Giant—roots that spread

a hundred acres, forty thousand

separate trunks that live and die

and live again for eighty thousand

years and counting. When the wind

blows, thirteen million pounds of tree

say, *Hush, hush, hussshhh*. I visited

and heard it. Why would it say more?

I tell you this because you need

to know. The Trembling Giant don't sweat

the saw. A man don't need to either.

I wasn't always like this. Time's

not necessarily kind, nor is

it necessarily on your side.

Example—you don't need to look

like ass right now but soon you do,

because that's life. And I was cooking

rice, he said, *I like your tits*.

I said, *They ain't for you, my friend*.

Sometimes I'm stupid, mostly smart—

I'm somewhere in the middle near

the front. I got a temper.

My plan was, *HAVE YOU SEEN THIS GIRL?*—

this fifteen-year-old Alison—

posters at every roadside stop

from Hollow Rock to San Diego.

My plan was, talk to Grandma rocking,

tell her . . . and listen, mostly listen.

Grandma said, *Went thataway,*

my Alison and her Bad Boy,

and pointed at the clouds.

Want to cry, driver? Grandma showed

me Alison's third-grade blue ribbon,

thumbtacked to the wall. *She stole it,*

Grandma said, *from Mary Tau*

that won. I never had the heart

to say I knew.

The kind of neediness kids feel,

some more than others, you could smell

it in the air.

            Was three a.m.,

the nighttime calm the way a night

can be, until an engine roared

and roared. She knew the car was coming

for her and her only. She dressed in blue

jeans and her daddy's flannel shirt

from the one picture Grandma kept—

yeah, Daddy loved his cocaine till

it killed him—and she slipped outside,

under a winter moon, the night

air filled with all the world. She did

not lock the door behind her, and

the boy she loved or thought she might

was sitting in the Chevy he

rebuilt with a V-8 because

he wanted them to hear him coming,

wanted them to hear him go.

They never had a destination,

Alison and her Bad Boy,

those winter nights. They meant to go

and did—the farms outside of town

the same till west of Memphis.

3

You know as well as I do, driver,

what you see from ten feet up—

the lives they live, the slowly dying,

handjobs, cigarette butts flaring

out of open windows, that

four-hundred-pound man crying in

his Cadillac a hundred miles

outside of Santa Fe, the dogs

in back, the million faces, none

the same and all the same. You know

after some time, it's all the same,

and in the sameness that's the danger—

that's where a young girl disappears.

West Memphis Flying J, across

the Mississippi, is Gomorrah,

City of the Plain. It's dust

and ash.

What you see from ten feet up,

idling on the lot—a girl—

there's no light darker than the flares

over the Flying J, across

the Mississippi, where a girl's

cries vanish like the wind across

the plain. You do not need to look

like ass because you wear pink shorts

or jeans and daddy's flannel when

you're fifteen years old stepping from

a Bad Boy's pickup truck so many

miles from home—but sooner or later

you do—you look like ass.

                     Is that

the way it happened, driver? What

promises made? The heat inside

your cab, not so unlike a kitchen.

Did you say, *Girl, I'll take you home?*

The lottery machine, the stamp

dispenser, the disposable phones

and calling cards, the dollar condoms,

one-way tickets from Flying J,

but you, the promises a man

like you can make, already eastbound,

cab as warm as toast. What girl

in her right mind, assuming that,

would turn you down?

All my life I'm doing things

they said I couldn't do. They said,

You won't have kids since Jimmy Acorn.

Tell that to my girl, still living,

thank the Lord, and reasonably

adjusted, which is more than you

or, if I'm honest, me. They said,

A truck's a beast ain't fit for ladies.

I said, *There ain't no other beast*

for me.

            They said,

Now, never mind it—girls that climb

inside a stranger's cab, they know

the smell of sulfur, the heat of fire

where worms will never die, by which

they meant, *That young girl must've known*

what she was getting into. Now,

here I am and here you are.

Tell me a story, I'll tell that story

back—names, dates unchanged. Describe

a stretch of highway, I'll dream that stretch—

eighteen wheels, twelve gears, five axles

turning, fifteen gallons of oil

to keep it clean. I'm floating gears,

tailing from Nashville, hauling forty

tons. I remember everything.

Oh, driver, I remember you.

What I saw—West Memphis night,

cold the way spring nights turn when

you think your love is here to stay—

the pickup V-8, humble like

a sleeping, breathing from twin tailpipes—

the door swung open like a mouth

and out came little Alison,

running, already running, barefoot—

why a girl'd be barefoot on

a Mississippi River night

in April defies common sense.

I knew from ten feet up, that's what

I saw—defiance. Bad Boy rolled

out on his side. Alison ran

but where's a girl like her to run?

I saw your truck roll out across

the headlights in the rain, the dark

swallowing steel and rubber.

4

Spring in Tennessee—the morning

after freezing rain falls—sun

on new-broke earth—and seven roads

run east from Memphis. What's a girl

to do?

The buzz of homeward bound—that mix

of hope and dread—I've felt it. Was

she tapping to the music that played

in Bad Boy's car and played and played

in her memory still—she worried it

might play forever? What the box knife?

What the glove? You daddy-talked

her out across the new-broke fields,

soil glistening silver in the sun?

Everything glistens in April sun.

And me?—I carry myself all

my life like *Don't you fuck with me*.

I carry myself like I got

something to do. I ain't no kind

of movie hero. If you want

a savior, try Jesus.

They found the bones inside the wrecked

barn past the creek—the rotten beams

and walls whistling in the wind,

a bale of rotten hay, and bones.

They said the tooth marks were coyote—

gave some peace to Grandma—said

some evidence of crow, but said

the rest was too far gone to know.

       Her ninth-grade teacher said,

Oh Alison oh Alison.

The Prospect Baptist preacher said,

Our Alison, like all God's lambs,

has come back to the fold—sooner

or later, we all come back to the fold.

But Bad Boy, when they found him crazed

on angel dust in Little Rock,

said nothing they could understand.

I'll tell you a short story, driver—

Her name was Alison. The end.

The longer version tells you more

and nothing more. *You* know the parts

no one else knows, the parts she didn't

know herself until you, and

by then it was too late. A girl—

she's out here by herself. The signs

are everywhere, but how is she

to know? On a West Memphis night

in April there's no hope—there's barely

Jesus. Anything can happen,

you put yourself out there like that,

if you ain't used to the life.

                        Stay in the light.

Try not to talk to people. Don't

ever climb in a stranger's cab.

There ain't no net.

5

They bagged her bones, as dry as wood chimes.

They did the thing they do with teeth

and tagged her, couldn't say what kind

of death except the tooth marks and

the broken ribs and thighbone, which

a wolf or grizzly does but not

in Tennessee. They boxed her up

and there's a cemetery out

on Roundhouse Road three miles from where

she lived, with forty gravestones and

a flag when the wind blows—the wind

never blows on Roundhouse Road—

and what I liked when I brought daisies—

beside the graveyard, a transformer

station, a little thing to light

the local countryside but plenty

to make a passing trucker think

electric current runs through dirt

and bone and never dies. Would seem

a shame to let it die. I'm less

ashamed of what I've done than what

I haven't.

You were a shadow to me then,

a shade among long-bearded men

slinking from cabs to shit or shower,

eat a stack at Denny's. Your hand

that stays, your hand that strays—it finds

a young girl's thigh, your eyes a dozen

miles away, like pennies left

on tables, silver laid on eyes,

gone a hundred fifty miles

before you blink, before you think

you're gone, before you remember where

you've been.

You know to leave the cab doors locked.

You know the truck stop whores by name.

You pop the locks and let the wind

and perfume—blind with sickness, blind

with ecstasy, or just plain blind.

You were a shadow then, a dark

spot in the dark, behind a windshield

glistening silver-black like new-

broke earth, an earth made of pure glass.

You should've locked your doors and, when

the girl ran barefoot on the lot,

stayed ten feet high, a bored, uncaring

God, ten thousand miles high, cold

in your cold heaven.

The only thing her grandma got

was turquoise earrings from among

the bones.

Some men like souvenirs. Not truckers.

The weight of bumper stickers from

the stops would pop a wheelie, keepsake

teaspoons dig canals. The world

is best passed through in tunnels. Why

the braid of blonde, brunette, and red,

the golden droplet like a charm?

Your cab so clean—you use some type

of product?—smells like happiness.

Why the silence, driver? Just

because you're a man don't mean your ass

can't get carried.

6

I-64 first dips, then climbs

in East Kentucky. Outside Grayson,

before the West Virginia line,

I got the flash—you ever get

that flash, driver?—when all you see

and all you cannot see comes clear?

You see through freezing rain, through dark,

and know the barefoot girl—you know her—

what happened, happens, and will happen.

I knew she'd die before you put

her body in the barn. I knew

the barn, the rotten wall, wind whistling.

I got the flash and knew.

I had a load of polymers—

American National Rubber—but

got off at Coalton, turned that load,

hauled six hours back through Tennessee.

The thing about a flash is it's

a flash and six hours later it

was gone and so was she and so

were you. I felt *despondent*—yeah,

a word I drove with thirty thousand

miles before I found the word

that followed, which was *hope*—because

the thing about a flash is it's

like lightning, never travels solo.

I was across the river, just

outside of Grand Forks, fueling at

the Eastside Travel Plaza, out

on Highway 2. There's nothing much

to see in North Dakota—that's

the point. From blindness insight, pupils

dilating in the night—the flash

so bright I had to leave the pump

and stare up at the sky with all

its dark forever. What I saw

was Alison's pink sneaker tumbling

out of Bad Boy's pickup, like

it needed to hop after her.

Pink memory like that—I had

to question, after forty days

and twenty thousand miles of crud

and soap, how much I trusted my

own eyes from ten feet up, through all

that dark, and I'd been wanting like

an aching for something pink.

I called the Flying J and talked

to Nightshift Benjy—said, *I lost*

my shoe. He said, *What kind of shoe?*

I said, *How many lost shoes do*

you get? He said, *You'd be surprised.*

One time, we got a crate of socks.

I said, *It's pink. The shoe is pink.*

He said, *Hold on*—and came back—*Sure,*

we got one pink.

Seventeen hours from North Dakota

to Tennessee. Bobtailing does

fifteen. I can't say why I needed

that pink shoe, why, when Manager Benjy

dug it out from Lost & Found—

like *What's your problem, hauling ass*

cross country for a pissed-up shoe?—

why I would carry it, the way

a preacher carries the communion

First Sundays, straight to the cornfield cops,

and say, *This is her body, this*

her soul. I tell you, corncob cops

don't care for lady truckers no more

than you do, driver. *What the hell,*

are we to do with this? they said.

I told them, *Watch the video—*

Flying J's got a name and half

a reputation. Look for a girl

streaks barefoot to a trucker's arms—

that's Alison. The cornfield cops

said, *Bones was all and turquoise earrings.*

Why do you want to mess our floor?

You take that shoe back outside when

you go. Go on now, go.

                    I went.

I put the pink shoe in a box

I keep beneath my bed at home,

with photos of my daughter. I

go on and on. I swear, sometimes

I wish I'd shut the hell up.

7

When I visited with Grandma,

she didn't want the pink shoe either.

She said, *Life's long and hard and maybe*

fifteen years is quite enough.

I said, *The man is hunting and hunting.*

She said, *Then let him hunt and hunt.*

What's it to me? I never hit

another woman, though one time

I did, then dropped my hands, my fists,

let Grandma close her rocking eyes,

and asked her, *What did you do to make*

her run? She said, *It wasn't me*

made Alison the way she was—

a hundred things, not least her mom

and dad. She went from bad to bad

and, when that boy came calling, went.

Yeah, Alison was lonely like

the rest of us, and maybe it

was time.

                       I visited again

in August, said, *I'm driving all*

Michael George

these miles, and Alison's ghost rides

shotgun, the way some truckers strap

stuffed animals or get a dog—

not much for conversation, but

someone that listens. Maybe it's guilt.

Maybe it's love, though I can't say

why it would be—it surely feels

like love. And Grandma rocked and rocked

and said, *You're spooking me.* I said,

You ever notice those who talk

the most get nowhere?

Third time, in late October, before

the bridges iced, she said, *Why do*

you care? Why can't you let her lie?

I said, *Why do you scratch an itch?*

Why does a dog go in heat? She said,

That ain't an answer. Truth was—can

I tell it to you, driver?—I

was lonely. Home, a hole I needed

to stay out of—the photos and

the shoe, like talking to the dead,

like voices in my head. I cut

around the city on the ring road.

I'll tell you a secret, driver—when

I was a child, I found a crow

chick fallen from its nest. Dead

but still warm in the summer sun.

I tore the feathers from its body,

peeled the skin, and pinched out bone

by bone. I tell you I ain't proud

of what I did but don't deny

I did. I thought those bones were magic,

thought if I found the words or sounds,

the right ones, I could stop time, thought

I could rise weightless from the ground

and visit places from my dreams.

A child, I was a child.

Did you feel magic in her bones?

Did you think time would stop? Did you

think eighty thousand pounds of cargo

would drop and you'd float free? I ask

because I need to know, the way

you need to know if someone that

you love loves *you*.

8

       I dreamed from outer space—

thousands of trucks, snailing across

your face—*your* face, driver. I couldn't

see your eyes under the treads.

I couldn't see your lips, your teeth

under the treads, and when I woke,

chill-sweating, naked, blanket on

the floor, I knew I'd tear your feathers,

peel your skin. I'd pinch your bones.

Now don't be frightened, driver. I'm

not done with you. We've many miles

to go before we—much unfinished.

Driver, the whole world's dangerous,

especially for women because

motherfuckers will try our ass.

We learn to keep our doors locked, stay

away from other truckers' cabs.

There's truck stops where we haul on past.

Restaurants are best because

of crowds. Strip clubs are good because

they have security. We never

park in shadows, never at

a place like *this*. No, nothing good

can happen at a place like this.

Hushed voices from another room—

no one's coming for you, driver.

No one will hear you because it can

get really loud. You gotta hold

your own.

I never knew

a trucker didn't have a reason.

You say you loved her as you held

the barrel to her head? Her bare

feet made you hard? And did you beg

for understanding as you pulled

the trigger? The world's unfair—you know

it and I know it. If you want

a second chance, you're dumb. You don't

look smart. You passed your second chance

outside Topeka. She held a sign.

It said, *Please help! God Bless!* She still

had teeth, a few. You know how that

worked out.

9

　　The way you think it was

it never was. The way you think

it will be, it's unlikely too.

I-95 from Boston down

to Jacksonville, a thousand miles—

I-10 from Jacksonville across

to LA, that's two thousand plus—

I-5 from LA to Seattle is

another thousand—and I-90,

Seattle through to Boston's three thousand—

round and round and round and round,

the inside portions soft as soft

but still can break your teeth.

　　　　　　　I tell

you this about New Mexico,

outside Las Cruces where I-10

bends west—I stopped for two long weeks

at a ten-buck-a-night motel,

which I do sometimes when I'm low.

The desert wind had shrunk and warped

the room door so the bitter light

of afternoon shined through three sides.

The window AC tore at the dark

all night, and still the room was hot

enough to fire my clay. I tell

you, driver, because it's something you

should know if we go further. No,

it ain't the clap. It's worse. I woke

up after those two weeks of hot

New Mexico nights, the bitter light

around the door, the bitter air

stinging me like sweat in a wound,

and, driver, I felt *good*.

                            I tell

you this—outside of Rapid City,

the *South Dakota Air and Space*

Museum, where I stop, or places

like it, when I'm feeling numb,

they have an Aviation Hall

of Fame with names of South Dakotans

who marked the sky the only way

they could and keep on living, which

was temporarily, and someone

in South Dakota thinks we should

remember.

                         I tell

you this about Nevada, Kansas,

Carolina—North and South—

there is no hole or hollow, no

motel or storage where a man

like you is safe from a woman like me.

My daddy said my rage would cause

me trouble someday. He was right.

10

I'm almost out of breath. I need

a good night's sleep. I need a shade

tree, but I've never found that tree.

I hope that when we're done I find it.

I haven't slept a good night since

young Alison. And breathing? Hell,

the air's been thin.

I've little patience for the long

goodbye. If you want tears, you'd best

look for them on the other side.

The man you've been—I've little patience.

The space you take—the road ice melts

once you've gone past. The last of you

should've died off a long time ago.

Last time

I drove through Tucson I bought earrings—

turquoise for your grave. I know

a barn, a wind-scoured place, where snow

blows through the cracks in winter and

the summer sun smells like scorched hay.

Michael George

I know a man whose bones hang heavy

with meat, sour sweat on bloody clothes.

I know that when you're naked, driver,

when you're skinned and pinched, a pile

of wet bones, truck stops still will smell

like bleach, like bodies caving in,

like fifteen-year-old girls who climb

in other cabs than yours. I know

that when your bones are summer dry,

reed hollow in the summer sun,

and barn rats drag a knuckle, foxes

filch a rib, and all the rest

is dust or will be, night will be

as dark, the rocking chair will rock,

and drying tears will mark their roads

with salt.

I'm tired of talking, driver, tired

of hurting, tired. If healing is

a lie, what's left but words to tell

your story round and round and round,

until you pass out, Dexedrine

making you see rabbits on

the road—or else you die—you pass

out or you die?

        If I take out the oil
rag, will you tell a story? We
have pliers and a saw. We don't
have time for lies.

Michael George

THE LIBRARIAN

1

I read it all but mostly local

history, biographies,

and novels set in China or

Louisiana—and line the books

on metal shelves that look like cotton

drying racks.

When books drop through the book return,

I smell the garlic, cigarettes,

and cooking oil of life—the quiet

suffering, and sugar, so

much sugar. I smell my neighbors' dreams

and fears—the pancreatic cancer

that killed young Jenny Vine—the German

shepherd Dennis Christensen

surprised his kids with after reading

up on breeds—the fuel-line trouble

Finley Jacobs fixed himself

before he sold his beat-up Ford—

and Vicki Holmes's fantasies

of ranch hands if "Talk Dirty to

Me, Cowboy" and "Rough Rider" are

a clue.

The funny thing is, as a kid

I hated books. When Janet hired

me for the job, she told me, *You'll*

learn secrets that'll dizzy you.

That did the trick.

When I was barefoot and eleven,

Miss Jensen gave me "Little House"

and told me, *Ruth, you'll see yourself*

in here. I opened up and all

I saw was ink. I took the book

home, tore the pages out,

and floated them on Cypress Creek.

I lied and told Miss Jensen Jeffrey

did it. Even when Dad whipped him,

Jeffrey never spilled.

     Like many other creatures,

I didn't understand the way

a mirror works—or understood

but didn't see the reason girls

would bother. Do mouths in a reflection

eat? Does the skin feel? Ears hear?

A long time passed before I learned

the answer—*Yes.*

Long before I realized mirrors

know things breathing people don't—

and when I was a girl and skipping

barefoot through the cotton fields

on June days when the blossoms shaded

pink, and thought the world was mine

and I the world's, with no one watching—

I lied to myself the way I lied

to Miss Jensen.

And if Miss Jensen walked in now

and asked a recommendation, I'd

give her a book on Sichuan frogs

or something untranslated from

Chinese—or maybe Mongolian

geology, and say, *You'll see*

yourself in here.

          My attitude

about a library is *Never*

whisper, but libraries have rules,

and even if the rules are lies,

well, lies are secrets too, and so,

although I'd have the kids who come

in after school take off their shoes

and run the aisles like Hemingway

from bulls or stand on desks and tables,

sounding their barbaric yawps,

I tell them, *Hush*.

I want to slip them books that make

them blush—and say, *You'll see yourself*—

I want to show them how a page

can float down Cypress Creek or light

on fire and never leave its binding

but point them to Ten Recommended

Books for Children and tell them, *Hush*

now, hush.

Michael George

2

Daddy left forty acres and

the house to me and forty acres

to Jeffrey—*That's how cotton grows,*

tap root systems twice as long

below as what you see above,

he said before they took him for

the final time. *I mean for it*

to be this way.

Jeffrey said he'd sell his half,

including what we shared—the picker,

the module builder, and the Massey

Ferguson from Granddad, red

the way a tractor should be red.

I said, *You don't sell patrimony.*

We're in those gears. Our blood is caked

in the paint.

He said, *No blood of mine.*

                                   I bought

his half, and now it rusts outside.

Huntersville is cotton fields

and timberland, and Jeffrey—his

eyes stared across the neighbor's fence.

He wanted what he couldn't have,

and when he couldn't have it he

grew angry—many men like that

in Tennessee. He didn't like

the spindle or the gin. He didn't

care for soybeans. Southern Concrete

Products needed men to pour

the precast septic tanks, but Jeffrey

couldn't see his way to that.

He wanted something where he felt

the sun.

Mother medicated him

when she met daddy, gave him to

her sister when they married, brought

him home for good when I was born—

a family sewn together with

old threads and new.

He took to sleeping in the barn

when Mother let him—five years old

when I was born, and *half a goat*

already, Daddy said, *Ha, ha,*

a boy needs leather, or he'll bleed.

      The heat in cotton barns

on August afternoons combusts

if you forget to spin a fan,

but Jeffrey came out cool as dew.

We should've known. And Daddy traced

his pallid skin with his brown fingers,

slow, as if Jeffrey's whiteness was

disgusting in a man or child.

Mother had another man

before she came to Tennessee

but never spoke of him in all

her years, though you could sense him in

her eyes, the way she looked across

the fields before the picking, when

the bolls were fat as autumn clouds.

If she saw anything of him

in Jeffrey, she blinked and turned away.

And Huntersville's a patch of land

between the Hatchee River, south,

and Forked Deer River, north,

where pavement's a pretension. What

chased Mother from that other man

must have been tragedy or fury.

Daddy caught her as she ran,

and though she sometimes sniffed the wind

as if she feared approaching menace,

she seemed peaceful other times

and even sang.

3

The summer nights when Jeffrey and

the other boys played baseball out

at Pope Park on Westover Road—

the streetlights buzzing yellow on

the diamond, shadows staining on

the grass beyond—the sky hung thick

and black and reassured a girl

that nothing changed. The woods outside

the chain-link knew their place, and I

knew mine.

There was a time when girls as brown

as I were prey for boys like Jeffrey.

The only reason other men

let Daddy live was Mother was

nobody's daughter—and he stopped

her wandering from house to house

and breaking windows.

The truth is Jeffrey suffered most,

a skinny child and frail where frail

gets held down in a pail. But watch

a drowning kitten and you'll see

a sight they'll talk about on Sunday—

the devil in its brittle bones,

and if your hands come out untorn,

you're wearing picking gloves.

On summer mornings when the bitter

odor of cut weeds—the racket

of chickens by the barn—the sun

beating through bedroom windows—a truck

thrumming a mile away—and then

the distant bells from Holly Grove—

the sounds and smells a world makes when

it lasts forever—Jeffrey cried

out then, a screaming song

and Daddy after him—the trouble

Jeffrey found at half past dawn.

       The way the land

bends in West Tennessee is like

an axle rod which, only when

you line it with your eye, reveals

its years of weight. You see it in

the backs of aging men who drive

the spindle pickers when they climb

down, pinch the cotton from a boll,

and hold it in their palms—the slope

of time from when we worked the fields

by hand.

I've read the histories—I knew

them long before I learned to read.

When Shedrick Pipkins buried men

ten miles from us on Britton's Lane

in 1862, where men

fell fighting, the smell spread wide across

the land and ruined that year's crop,

the little that remained, the stink

so deep they couldn't purge it with lye.

We never got the forty acres—

knew better than to ask—although

some families left for Promise Land

in Dickson County where they made

a life. Not us. We stayed and bent

our backs.

When Great-granddaddy bought the farm

he'd crushed his bones for, cotton brokers

halved the bale price.

                    Now,
    on summer days, with Jeffrey gone,

    the clouded sky seems to weigh twice

    as much as the unplanted fields.

4

When I was nine, I found a pine

snake with no head inside the barn,

and Daddy said, *One time I saw*

an owl decapitate a cat

to get the brains.

        I said, *A cat*

is not a snake.

        He said, *Rats then.*

I said, *Do rats use knives?*—because

the snake had Jeffrey's knife beside it.

Next time, a chicken we called Cindy—

head, feet, most of her feathers, gone.

Foxes, Daddy said, *or else*

raccoons.

By that point Sheriff Coates had come

to talk. He said, *It may be none*

my business but I warn you now

before it is. There's troubles you

see coming—some you don't—I've seen

this kind before though never quite

like him. If I was you, I'd change

the scenery—or else the locks.

Mother's sister lived in Hot Springs,

and Daddy said, *We have two choices.*

one is County Juvenile.

I'd never gone to any state

but Tennessee, and nor had Jeffrey

since he could remember. Four

of us in Daddy's Dodge Mirada,

singing all the way to Memphis,

where we crossed the Mississippi,

Daddy pointing how the truss

bridge struts connected to the road

and saying, *Strength is in the space*

between the cables—don't forget

that, you'll be fine.

And Mother saying,

What the hell is that supposed

to mean?

Then Daddy stopped the car

above the river, saying, *You think*

the strength is in the steel—and steel

is strong—but most, it's in the things

you never see.

And Mother turned,

as cars and trucks and buses split

around us blowing horns, and said,

Your daddy thinks he smart,

but he's a big bowl of thin soup,

which may have been the cleverest thing

she ever said.

So Jeffrey lived

two years with Aunt Corrine before

she sent him back. I heard her on

the phone say, *Never, never, never,*

then Jeffrey rode home on a bus.

At sixteen he'd become a man

in body if not mind. He wouldn't

tell me what the problem was

but said the girls in Arkansas

were whores.

When Mr. Jinny's

brindle shepherd disappeared,

no one came knocking—the nights were quiet.

Then someone ripped the copper from

the kitchen at Deliverance

House of Prayer on Friday night

and then Lane Chapel Saturday,

so worshippers drank water out

of plastic jugs on Sunday morning.

At first nobody noticed when

a '76 Trans-Am drove off

from Clement's Cars though skid marks made

a trail down Brownsville Highway to

the tree where Jeffrey wrecked it.

          He met a girl

in Gadsden who was half as bad

as he. If laws of averages

applied they'd be all right, and we

all hoped it wouldn't be addition.

What they did or didn't do

the night she died nobody knew,

but Mother swore he was at home.

The sheriff questioned him, and he

seemed chastened and a bit afraid.

There're times when looking at the truth

hurts more than staring at the sun.

5

                    The edges of

the wooden porch rot last. The spots

where we set flowerpots grow soft

as flesh. Paint flecks accumulate

along the windowsill, wash down

the side, and fade like river stones,

then sand, then nothing. The barn shades red

to gray, as blood in wind and rain,

and cedar splinters peel as thick

as strips of scab on the horse that rakes

her hide along the barbed wire fence.

The B. Wright doll that Grandma gave me

is losing her hair,

a black-thread halo on the shelf.

I'm down to seven drinking glasses

from the set of twelve. They paved the road

once years ago—you'd never know it.

Bindings break, and when I opened

a Yeats biography, a herd

of silverfish, pig-fat on glue,

rushed out across the counter top.

Janet said, *Things fall apart.*

We laughed. Perhaps we shouldn't have.

6

Late autumn, after harvest and

the clearing, men with muzzleloaders,

hunting something thick they feel

inside—and though they smoke or chew,

they taste blood iron on their tongues—

trudge shin deep through stubble fields

as if the land belongs to God,

and though I stand in the window watching,

they neither knock nor nod but set

their heavy boots in dirt until

they reach the woods and disappear

like smoke from rifle barrels or

the smoky vanishings of deer.

Until the Indian Removal Act

of 1830, Chickasaws

lived here, and now they don't.

On afternoons when cold rain falls,

the men seek shelter—twice I've found

them hiding on the porch, and once

a pair broke off the work-shed door.

When I was

Michael George

a girl and skipping through June cotton,

Daddy told me, *You better run*

your fastest—never blink. The truth

is some wounds never heal. The truth

is all the lies I've read in books

are only lies, and they distract

me for a while but nothing more.

Although I have a sense of place,

this place was never mine. The truth

is sooner or later you must blink

or you'll go blind.

                          The truth

is Daddy took his shirt off and

I saw the scars. Skipping is fun

until you realize it's rhymed tripping.

                          The truth

is Mother was a whore—it hurts

to say it, but it's true. The truth

is winter follows autumn follows

summer follows spring, and even

retarded children know that. The truth

is I prefer the beautiful—

I'll lift up stones to find it. The truth

is when they talk of days of rest

I don't know what they mean. The truth

is I don't mind the dust. The truth

is spring days smell like death before

they smell like birth or life. The truth

is I love nothing more than where

I am.

                             The truth

is Mother died, then Daddy died,

then Jeffrey sold his share and bought

a truck, and I sold off the horse

and chickens, fixed the window screens.

I'd rather be alone. The truth

is I don't care so much for truth.

7

We almost killed each other on

the morning Jeffrey said he'd go.

Since Daddy died, we lost a bit

each year—the price of cotton down

and falling. Jeffrey hated losing—

I asked him why he figured leaving

meant he'd win. He made a deal

to sell his half the land and barn,

and told me if I knew what's best

I'd do like him. I asked, what use

is half a cotton farm without

a barn to keep machines and seed?

He said, no use at all as far

as he could tell. I said I'd die

or see him die before I'd lose

the house. That's when he pulled the knife.

I'd watched him gut a doe. He'd hung

it from a rafter, hind legs spread.

He'd zipped the belly down and scraped

the skin until it peeled the way

a ripened peach skin peels—too loose,

not loose enough.

He'd hacked the forelegs at the joints.

A finger in her anus, he'd

cut a loin and then the other.

He'd used a saw to split the spine

and separate the shanks and round.

Minutes later, he'd cut out

the liver, shaved a silky piece,

and laid it on his tongue.

I grabbed the kettle from the stove—

I'd brain him if he took a step.

He laughed and put away the knife

and hugged me, laughing, and—he didn't

hide it—he was hard as hard.

He said, *Ruth, honey, you and me*—

just that, just *you and me*.

He bought the truck with what he got,

a Freightliner Cascadia—

the best, he said, for men who want

to sleep and eat and drive. He said

he'd see the world and he'd be free.

I saw

him after that once, twice a year—

and sometimes people bringing books

back said they saw him passing through.

One time in August when I went

to Mother's grave, I could've sworn

I smelled him in the heat, and then

I found a silver necklace with

a pendant chip of amethyst

set where the cutter cut her name—

and thought of cats that leave dead shrews

or sparrows on the doorstep as

a gift of love or obligation.

Three days later I received

a card from St. Paul, Minnesota,

where he said he'd dropped a load—

I felt I knew but couldn't swear.

The truth is distance has a grip—

you feel it in the chest and head

and muscles. Many nights alone,

I listened to the wind or rain

as if the voices speaking through

the walls and floor could tell me where

I'd left the key. I wondered if

a truck as black as two a.m.

inside a house was coming home

or leaving still, or if there was

a difference.

                    The truth

is I loved Jeffrey.

8

West Alley Smokehouse, where we held

the Christmas party for town workers,

had southern fried fish platters all

year round. I felt the stares and heard

the whispers, knew the averted gaze.

Dana Tomley dabbed her lips

and left her table and her lunch

to ask me what the men were doing

out on Jeffrey's forty—which

was what we called it still, although

nine years had passed since Jeffrey signed

the deed.

      I said, *What men?*—I'd worked

all morning shelving books.

                  She said,

White-hooded men, and Becky Walters

chittered like we all knew what

white-hooded men did to brown women.

Dana Tomelson said, *Hush,*

and asked again, *White-hooded men,*

and Sheriff Coates is there?

              I lied—

I'm sure I don't know what you mean,

and sipped my tea, to keep from choking.

I knew the pine snake with no head.

I knew the chicken no raccoon

or fox had killed. I knew the bloody

iron and salt of organ meat

on Jeffrey's tongue. I knew the smell

of Jeffrey when he seemed to be

a thousand miles away.

I'd never had a premonition,

but reading and arithmetic

sometimes astonished me with sudden

recognitions, dim or bright.

I drove home, and—at Freeman Lane—

I stopped and vomited my fish.

Becky Walters had gotten it right—

the sheriff's men had come in white

hoods, boots, and gloves, and Sheriff Coates

stared at the sky, as if he wanted

rain to wash the land away.

9

Off-season hunters had found the bones.

They scented death and followed it

the way you hate to but you must.

The flesh was gone—the muscle and blood

decayed and drained into the dirt.

Sheriff Coates, who knew these things,

asked me Jeffrey's whereabouts.

I said, *A boy grows up, becomes*

a man—Why can't you let him leave?

They showed the pictures on the news,

and no one mentioned Jeffrey's name

but I could hear it in the silence.

They said the bones came from a girl

named Alison who ran away,

but then the story cracked—it seemed

some other places had found bones

with gnawings like these ones.

10

The coming autumn, when they put

a lock back on the barn, I broke

it with a shovel, went inside,

and sat on the rough dirt. I sniffed—

and got on hands and knees and sniffed.

I couldn't smell the girl in life

or death, but felt I might be her,

who couldn't find herself—both there

and gone.

       For hours and hours I let

the anger grow, and then I let

it go. Sometimes it's time to let

it go.

THE DETECTIVE

1

Fifty, sixty gunshots. Glass,

aluminum, blood, plastic beads.

The witness—Black, six one, two ten—

lungs huffing—said, *My boys were like,*

get down, get down, get down.

         I said,

You need a paper bag to breathe in?

Great big man like you needs air

unless you want a heart attack.

       He said,

You don't expect Afghanistan

on Monday morning.

    I said, *I don't expect a man*

like you to hide behind a dryer.

    He said, *A man like me?*

         I said,

Two bodies and a third one hardly

living—you without a scratch.

You own a gun?

He said, *A man*

like me don't do his laundry? Is

that bigotry or just plain stupid?

Darla said,

A scare like this'll soil your shorts.

You need a dollar for a load?

He huffed and huffed and said,

I need to get my stuff.

She said, *Unlikely—*

and waved at Charlie Redman, who's

the evidence technician—said,

Good Morning, Charlie—and he waved—

We've gotta take your clothes. Theirs too—

she meant the bodies of the dead—

male African-American,

five six, in sweatpants that said "Chill,"

the other, female, white, red-haired,

and kind of cute—*It's how it works,*

although that kind of sucks for you,

a clean guy out to wash his pants—

she gave him that deep look she gives—

What'd you say about that gun?

      Well, Jesus Christ, he said. *You got*

me, sister—offering his wrists.

They took the one who lived across

the bridge to Presley Trauma, where

they stabilized and sewed him, left

the bullets in his arms and leg,

but operated on his lung,

and three days later when he talked

he said he'd screwed the girlfriend of

a guy high up in the Vice Lords.

When Shelby County shot him dead,

it all worked out. We told the man

we busted at the laundromat

we went too far—apologized

in person how we did since all

the bad publicity and shame

when the West Memphis Three got back

their freedom eighteen years too late.

You wrap it up and tie a bow,

and it's a birthday party all

year long.

2

        They say

West Memphis is a dying town,

the population down to where

we were in 1965.

You count on toes and fingers, heck,

we're dying, but the quality

of life is what I look at, and

it's high. At Southland Greyhound Park,

on "Ho Ho Hotseat" Fridays since

the renovations, slots ring out

like Easter church bells—people drive

from everywhere.

        I'd never denigrate

a neighbor, but I wouldn't live

across the river. Tennessee

is fine for Tennesseans, but

we have a sense of humor and

the only working diamond mine

in the United States. There's much

more than you'd guess. On Thursday nights,

my friend and housemate Jim and I

have tickets to the Theatre.

I say don't advertise it, but

he says, *It's family-style fun*

and *Anyone who thinks that way*

is halfway there himself. He's been

a city councilman the last

eight years. I trust him on these things.

There's Riverside for stock car races

April through the fall. For drinks

it's mostly Frasure's Backdour Club.

Jim laughs at that. I say, *Don't be*

a damned cliché—but Tuesday night

is steak night, Thursday's karaoke,

Fridays ShotGunBillys shred

some ZZ Top. They blow the roof

off, nothing left for Charlie's bags.

At the West Memphis Welcome Center,

all you do is take a leak—

the restrooms known for cleanliness,

all credit to Holmes Hammett, who's

Executive Director at

the Chamber. And Old Airport Club

is fine for pool, and someday they'll

repave. You'll find me in the stands

in my blue booster t-shirt yelling,

Go! Blue Devils!

3

   A-fucking-nother one,

Chief said. He's a good man when drunk.

when sober he buys all the words

the mayor and Holmes Hammett talk

since the West Memphis Three and all

the crap that's flowed—it's almost choked

the Mississippi, surely clogged

our throats and ears—and then he says,

community-wide partnership.

a model of professionalism.

Our service is our greatest product.

Heck, if you don't want your kid

accused of Satanism, then

don't name him Damien, right?

I get pissed off when people think

I have no sense of humor. Sure,

it hurts—get used to it—grow up.

But sometimes it feels personal,

a blade that pries between the skin

and nail and finds the nerve.

Chief gave me the report—

a family of five was driving

through to Dallas in the sleet

and, hungry for a bag of Lays,

pulled over at the Flying J.

They saw a girl—or thought it was

a girl, it could've been a long-

haired boy—the night was black and wet,

the man's hands full of chips and kids,

the woman tired—run barefoot to

a semi, disappear inside.

The semi drove away. The man

felt something wrong, the woman not

so sure but stayed an extra minute

to tell Security her story.

She said, *I'd hate to find out later*

and know I drove away without.

I gave it back to Chief—*It's Riley's.*

Missing kids, not homicide.

Chief shoved it back and said, *I've got*

a bad, bad feeling.

You should drink

a better brand, I said.

                        He said,

If you had half my troubles, closed

his office door, and left us all

to suffer for his sins.

Security had nothing when

I asked, though I asked very little.

Many reasons girls—and boys

who look like girls—might climb inside

a semi, most involving cash

and pimps. A problem, sure, but not

my problem. Spread the load, I say.

There's other shoulders wide as mine.

The guard shrugged when I told him he

was wasting time and said, *The man*

seemed real shook up.

        Darla's mostly cool

about the work. My motto's *Save*

your treads for when you need them. Keep

your tank half-full. You act like life's

a mile-wide track, you'll likely slide

out when you hit the bend. But when

she saw Chief's paper on my desk,

describing this and that about

the missing kid, she got all anxious

like she'd reached across the counter

when the clerk was busy with

the cigarettes. I always thought

she was a lesbian, but moments

like this I believed she had

more history she didn't share,

the kind you smell in dripping sweat

and hear in quaking voices. I

said, *Darla, honey, what's the shakes?*

She never liked the *honey* part

and didn't care for *shakes*. She shook

the paper in my face and said,

Why wasn't I informed of this?

I said, *A teenage prostitute*

at Flying J? You want a call

for each of them, you'll never sleep,

a letter for each horny trucker,

you'll break the postman's back.

She said, *I've got a bad, bad feeling.*

As these things

do, this one went away. But it

was like a locust or a seed.

4

      We built a wall around

the backyard garden where Jim grows

hydrangeas—brick to keep the deer

and rabbits out. May mornings in

West Memphis, clover blooms in alleys,

and for a couple weeks the air

is clear. So when Chief said, *A body—*

Avalon and Broadway by

the Walgreens—looks like overdose—

I breathed the clear air deep.

                    I knew

the man behind the Dumpster. In

a town this size you do. We went

to high school, hung out, shooting hoops—

a friend I never thought of much

and, when we graduated, thought

of less until I didn't think

of him at all, and when we met

at Baskins Tire and Service or

at Kroger, we said, *Hey*, but didn't

stop to talk, and now it seemed

my memory of him and how

he cared about himself ran side

by side through all the years, there was

so little left of him.

Although the day was warm, he wore

his winter boots and winter vest,

his blue jeans cinched around his waist

with a frayed leather belt. I crouched

beside him, prodded him a bit,

examined ankles, belly, arms,

and neck for needle marks—and thought

I recognized the belt, the big

brass buckle, though I shouldn't after—

then I realized I forgot

his name.

That night, Jim held me while I cried.

The boxwoods and the hollies in

the front grow greener every year,

and when we lop them till they look

like sheep at shearing, they grow greener.

The poplar and the maple in

the side yard do their work without
complaint. When Susan split and took
our son to Fayetteville, I shrank.
We knew it had to end, and when
it did, I thought I'd feel a lightness
and liberty, but mostly I
felt sad. Then I met Jim, and, heck,
I never would've thought.

I wouldn't call it growth but it's
a change. I talk to Susan twice
a month. She says she's found a joy
in life she never had with me.
Our boy?—He's started talking now
but doesn't know the difference.

For anyone who asks, Jim has
his room, I mine—and no one asks,
not lately, which keeps peace at home
and calm at work. We draw the shades
in front and back. Except at corners,
we have no streetlights on our stretch
of Roselawn Road. Heck, who am I
to judge? Beneath the carport, we

park side by side. I said no to

the Easter wreath.

After long enough, some scars

retreat below the skin, and pink

shows only when we sweat.

5

                            On June

the Fourth, a man whose given name

was John Theophilus—we called

him Cooter—died when Mrs. Larson

ran him over with her Buick.

We laughed since Mrs. Larson just

turned ninety-six, and Cooter was

a nasty bastard to both young

and old.

                            Next day,

a lady trucker in white jeans,

black leather jacket, cowboy boots

above her knees, blonde hair, burst through

the door and laid a beaten-up

pink sneaker on the lobby desk.

Chief said, *Now, what the hell?* We get

enough of lunatics inside

the city borders—we don't need

to bring in new ones from abroad.

The lady said, *I have a shoe—*

Chief said, *I see that clearly, ma'am.*

She said, *The girl it once belonged*
to I'm afraid for—

She told a story of that night

outside the Flying J—a girl

she saw run barefoot from a pickup—

a semitrailer driver whose

arms reached down to the pavement like

a clutch of tentacles, a pair

of claws, a father's hug. She told

of miles she'd driven, haunted by

that girl, and how she saw a flash

in Grand Forks, North Dakota—and

that's where she started losing us,

until she said, *I've got a bad,*

bad feeling, officers.

Chief said,

Well, damn, and disappeared inside

his office as he does when feeling

all the trouble in the world

but came back with a printout from

the state police, another from

the DOJ. He said, *A girl*

from Tennessee went missing on

an April night—last seen in jeans,

pink sneakers, and a flannel shirt.

        Well, holy cow, I said.

             Chief frowned

as if he learned he had a tumor

and said, *Last week they found her bones—*

the papers shaking in his hand,

some men not cut out for this work—

and told the trucker, *Sorry, ma'am,*

it seems you've come too late. Police

in Huntersville might want the shoe.

We don't. He looked as if he couldn't

stand its stink.

          The trucker said,

The man who did it—he was here.

Watch the video.

And Chief

said, *Darla, will you show the lady*

out?

6

5-5-1993.

Three eight-year-olds. Three feet, six inches.

Sixty-five pounds. Also names—

Steve Edward Branch and Christopher

Mark Byers and James Michael Moore—

the boys who died, their bodies in

a drainage ditch.

And eighteen, sixteen, seventeen—

the ages of three other boys

locked up for eighteen years.

West Memphis Three. Names—Jason Baldwin,

Damien Echols, Jessie Misskelley.

Chief didn't want to go back down

that road. A young man then himself,

he knew the boys the way I knew

the man behind the Walgreens Dumpster—

Terry Sheldon! Names come back.

When oil stains spread across the pavement,

innocence and guilt, the one

who spilled, the one who mopped, don't matter.

We all get dirty. Blood stains too.

For many years it was like that,

a TV game. The clue—"West Memphis."

The answer—"What's a triple murder?"

Then, around the time a stranger

could look us square without disgust,

they changed the game—"West Memphis"—and

"What's a rotten conviction?"—Double

points for "What is railroad justice?"

It's hard to love a town.

I said to Chief, *You told her right.*

The body, it's in Huntersville—

It's theirs. She came from Hollow Rock—

Not ours. The FBI will handle

interstate, and, sure, it might

be murky as the Mississippi

River between Arkansas

and Tennessee—and, heck, we make

our licenses reciprocal

instead of asking catfish where

they're from—that's common sense—but right

is right, and if we get involved

we run the risk. The prudent thing,

the cautious choice—that's what this is.

Chief said, *I suffer from depression,*

arthritis, and a hairy mole

on my left foot that worries me.

They used to call it getting old,

but I know right from wrong.

I said, *I'm glad to hear that, Chief.*

I strapped my pistol on and said

a prayer as soldiers do before

a war.

7

The preacher stood alone
inside his tent. I have a soft
spot in my heart for lonely men.
Suspicion too. I asked him where
he was all April—was he here?

He said,

In Mississippi, down along
the Delta, then in Baton Rouge.
Galatians Six. In early spring
I sow the seeds in warmer soil,
and in due season we shall reap.
And he that soweth to the spirit
shall of the spirit reap.

Then Darla flashed the picture, asked,
You seen this girl?
He held the picture
near and far. I thought I saw
the itching of a tear.
She ain't
the Virgin Mary, Darla said.

Michael George

Did you see her?—yes or no?

The preacher held the picture like

he'd make it his. *A lost child?* Then

the tear came. *When I was a boy,*

he said, *I knew a girl who looked*

like her, and loved her for a while.

But no, I never saw this one.

So, Darla searched his cargo van—

found Bibles, hymnals, thermoses,

a bag of weed she could've made

a point of, forks, knives, spoons, shampoo.

She climbed out and said, *Clean.*

I could

grow tired of saying sorry—I

said, *Sorry*, to the preacher, *We've*

been hypocrites.

He said, *God bless*

your soul, detective, so have I.

Jill Berenson,

the daytime manager, hung out

at Eagle Lanes when we were kids.

She bowled a spare, got pregnant, dropped

out—where the baby went we never

knew—but things turned out all right,

and sometimes after work she'd drink

at Frasure's Backdour Club when Jim

and I were there.

        I said, *Jill, honey,*

we have a real bad situation,

and asked to see their video.

We watched it on her office laptop,

and what we saw was nothing more

than we expected. A sleeting night.

A lens cleaned once some years ago.

A glaring, spread like cracking glass.

A wisp of drivers at the pumps.

A woman, man, and children shining

in crazed fluorescence as they went

inside. The cars and trucks slid in,

slid out, like phantoms lost in space

and time, like nothing solider

than dreams or hope. No girl ran barefoot—

no one scrambled from a pickup—

no one got sucked up inside

a semi cab.

        Darla smacked

the screen as if the camera

might lie.

    Jill said, *It reaches to*

a certain point. Beyond it, you

step off the edge.

        I hear her screaming,

Darla said. *I see her fall.*

8

A hole inside the hole inside.

When Jim first said he loved me, I

felt lighter than. I don't know science—

I don't know how things work in mind

or body, but I felt a lightness

as if the image of me on

a film disintegrated. It

felt bad. It hurt like nothing ever.

All I knew and all I thought—

as if my legs and arms were floating

or else the rest of me—across

and out. I can't blame others for

their misperceptions when my life

until that point—and when I saw

a hole and understood that holes

are . . . not an absence, more a way

that I unsee what's there because

if I acknowledge that the hole

inside the hole weighs nothing and

that nothing has the power to pull

me in, becoming everything—

I've always been a confident man,

always sure-footed. When I aim,

I hit my quarry. When Jim said

he loved me and I felt I loved,

I will admit, I was afraid.

           What I know

and what I don't are much too much

the same. A girl who falls into

a hole. A man who thinks he knows

the measure of himself. Or Chief

who digs a hole inside because

his brain's a shovel. I have come

to think, there's nothing else than holes.

9

Chief said, *Ask Jazzy.*

Nope, I said.

Jazzy—up by Marion—

does readings from her house, which backs

to railroad tracks. Some people swear

that when the freight trains pass, they feel

a supernatural tremble. They say

she's gotten some things right that aren't

explainable by other means.

I'd rather pray, I said.

And Chief

said, *First Assembly, First United,*

Holy Cross, Grace Baptist—Pick

your pastor.

Chief, I said, *I'd rather*

pray than waste the time, but praying's

wasting too—

Boy, he said, *I worry since*

your wife went back to Fayetteville.

I said, *The girl's a hole, you see?*

He said, *I don't see anything.*

I said, *You've got it now—the girl*
is in the nothing you can see.

He said, *You better cut that talk.*

I said, *The girl we're looking for*
is gone. She never was, or if
she was, we didn't know until
she wasn't. She was looking—as
we all are—for a thing she didn't
know, and when she found it, if
she found it, it was blacker than
a sleeting April night. It didn't
need to be, but was. For some
it's bright—for me—

Chief said, *I've heard the rumors—who*
you've been since Susan left you. Are
they true?

They're gone, I said. *Don't try to hold*

them here. The shoe the driver brought

us, pink as pink? You try to touch

it, and your fingers go straight through.

And you and me?—I jabbed him with

a finger in his chest—*We're gone*

too, never were, or if we were,

we weren't the ones we thought we were.

Then Chief was trembling and he roared

from somewhere in his hollow core,

Back off, Detective. What the hell—

you talk that shit—these holes and nothings,

gones and blacks and brights. Have you

forgotten who you are?

In fact, I said, *I never knew.*

He sighed and said, *Get Darla. Sign*

a car out. Talk to Jazzy. Pray

with pastors—say a prayer for me.

Go home and hold your boyfriend's hand.

Or meditate on nothing if

you'll find the answers there—but I

need answers, and if you can't find

them, tell me lies and let me sleep.

Hell of a world, and what do I

know anymore?

10

If you stay quiet for a while,

the crickets make the noise they used

to make—and people too. When June

became July, then August, traffic

rushed along the northern edge

of town all night and sometimes horns

would blast or loads would settle on

the truck beds, stirring us from sleep—

       And, if the wind

was right, the Union Pacific, rocking

Jazzy and her neighbors, rocked

us too, the gentlest cradle and

the gentlest song—

       And Tenmile Bayou,

under bridges, past the fields

and backyards, churches, factories,

and schools, was silent but on nights

when kids drank beer or shadows brushed

through scrub. We could've lived like that

without objection.

       Chief spent days and nights

behind his door, and if he called

me in, I said, *I'm on it, Chief.*

that seemed enough.

         Then Darla got

a taste for codeine syrup, went

on leave for twenty days, and came

back clean.

         And work was busy. In

West Memphis summers, that's routine.

A body in the ditch between

East Service Road and Motel 6—

we called it hit-and-run—a boy

who tried to climb the water tower—

accidental—drug-related

shootings on McCauley Drive.

         We couldn't find the driver, buried

the boy, and on the morning we

broke down the dealer's door we found

him with a needle in his eye

and a cut throat. It added up

to fifty-fifty for the season—

fine for us.

That fall,

when Jim got reelected to

the City Council, Reverend Stone

and six of his parishioners

waved signs on our front lawn. I aimed

a warning shot above their heads,

which, in another town, might cause

a ruckus.

Susan sent a picture of

our boy on Christmas—two years old,

a stranger to me—and I framed

it to remind me of the shape

of him.

Jim's backyard garden died

in the first freeze. He made a wreath

of the dead roses, and I hung

it on the door.

On Tuesday nights

in January, we ate steak

at Frasure's, Thursdays karaoke,

Fridays—heck, on Fridays we

stayed home.

Michael George

It could've gone like that

forever, but it never does.

The lady driver, back from where

she'd been, crashed through the station door

and said, *I've got some news for you.*

11

Like a lot

of first-time murderers she needed

validation for what she'd done,

as if erasing someone else

erased a part of her. She showed

her hands for confirmation like

a woman who had swayed a crowd,

and when we didn't clap, she seemed

to wonder if we saw her.

She wouldn't tell us who or where

he was, but said, *I'm tired of driving,*

tired of hurting, tired.

              Chief smiled,

as if he knew.

              We locked her in

a cell three nights and made the calls.

The FBI, the DOJ,

the sheriff came from Huntersville.

She told them, *There we were, and what*

use blaming? All those miles, exhaust

fumes blowing from our pipes, and in

a breeze the evidence of where

we'd been and where we'd go was gone.

The sheriff asked her, *Where's his body?*

Gone, she said.

I smiled, as if

I knew.

The FBI man asked,

And where's his truck?

A beautiful

machine, she said, *and valuable*

to men both bad and good.

The DOJ man asked,

What did you do?

She said, *Did he*

say, Girl, I'll take you home? Did she

say, Home's a place I've never known?

Then where's a girl like her to run?

I don't believe in destiny,

and if a trucking life has taught

me anything, it's there's no place

to run. She died for being where

she was, and maybe he did too.

We kept her locked up three nights more,

and then we let her out. She seemed

despondent when we said she had

to go as if she didn't quite

believe her words on destiny

and destinations.

                   Hit the road,

Chief said, *unless you've more to say.*

        Then Darla said, *There's animals*

that wander. You seem one.

           The lady's eyes

were full of tears she'd never cry.

She seemed to choke, as if the words

inside her would be spoken but

her muscles wouldn't speak.

I said, *I think I understand.*

She smiled as if I never would,
which meant I did.

        I walked her out,
and in the winter sun, I told
her when she drove through Arkansas,
we had a bedroom at my house
that we kept empty most nights, where
we'd promise her a stretch of sleep.
We couldn't give her love or peace.
We couldn't be the place or time
she looked for. But we had a roof
and walls, and if she came they would
be hers.

12

That night, Jim in my arms, and I—

a cold rain falling—I in bed,

sang a West Memphis lullaby

for the living and the dead—

Between the guilt and innocence

of children—by the dying field—

between the skip and trip of dance—

we can't recall the spoken word,

believing what is done is done—

the bone, the ligament, the joint

snapped or torn or wrenched and grown

over—calcified—a stunted

growth—as if we have no will

to break again and, breaking, turn

time back, reversing possible

articulations, making born

unborn, and wearing space as if

it is a jacket we can change

to fit the season, kicking off

a door that lacks a knob or hinge.

The child, if she was real, was real
the way that snow is—neither here
nor there, a freezing will
to being, melting in her hair

as she ran barefoot from her life,
and if the driver, whose thick arms
she found—if any arms—and if
that frozen driver, offering warmth,

was real, he too was gone already,
and when the blade—if any blade—
cut out his heart, denied his body,
his heart was ice, his body dead,

the blade a confirmation of
the facts—the ones that melt like ice—
and if the lady, in her love
or hatred, out of time and space,

was real, it's best to let her go
to other times and other spaces
where hatred and love—not here, not now—

have other bodies, other faces—

and if we need an answer—an end—
my love, my friend—provisional
or definite—the way light bends
might mean the answer isn't real,

and ends, a lie—but we might bend
the way the light bends, toward the dark
without succumbing to it, and
we might find rest at end of work—

in your arms, mine, in gardens in
the spring, and wreathes we hang on doors
when summer passes, in what's gone
if it was ever here—

if we see less and call it more—
if we hold one another, in spite
of now and then and here and there—
        Oh baby, we'll be right.

ABOUT MICHAEL GEORGE

Writing as Michael Wiley, Michael George is the author of eleven novels and two books of literary criticism. Recipient of the Best Novel Shamus Award for A Bad Night's Sleep as well as other prizes and nominations for his long fiction, he also publishes short stories, including "Where There's Love," selected for the Best Mystery Stories of 2022 anthology. His fiction focuses on crime, in Chicago, where he grew up, the Southeast, where he has lived for the past twenty-five years, and, as in Find Your Own Way Home, the spaces in between.

Having worked as an itinerant cherry picker, an attendant at an in-patient mental health facility, and a speechwriter, Michael is a professor of creative writing and literature at the University of North Florida.